MW01264914

Out with Consequences

A Journey out of Jehovah's Witnesses

Debbie L McDaniel

ISBN: 150330082X
ISBN 13: 9781503300828
Library of Congress Control Number: 2014921006
CreateSpace Independent Publishing Platform
North Charleston South Carolina

Dedicated to Crystal and Marley
My team, my family, my loves

Foreword

IN A WORLD CONTAINING A SEA OF RELIGIONS THERE SHOULD BE A MOMENT THAT COMES INTO ONES LIFE THAT THEY CAN SIMPLY FIND FAITH. MANY RELIGIONS MAKE THAT HARDER FOR ONES THAN GOD INTENDED IT TO BE.

THE FOLLOWING STORY CONTAINS EVENTS AS I REMEMBER THEM AND AS I SEE THEM CURRENTLY. THESE EVENTS WILL BE UPSETTING TO SOME AND FOR THOSE UPSETS THAT COME TO PEOPLE I LOVE, I AM SORRY.

PERHAPS CRIMES SHOULD NOT HAVE BEEN OVERLOOKED AS IF THEY WERE INSIGNIFICANT. PERHAPS HOMOSEXUALITY DOES NOT MAKE ONE A LESSER HUMAN BEING OR LESS DESERVING OF DIGNITY AND RESPECT. JUST PERHAPS. PERHAPS GAY INDIVIDUALS CAN, IN FACT, MAKE GOOD PARENTS. WHY NOT BE OPEN TO THE POSSIBILITY….

WHEN SHUNNING OF ANY INDIVIDUAL OCCURS, IT IS DAMAGING TO THEIR SPIRIT, SOUL AND ULTIMATELY TO THEIR BODY. THE WORST OF HARDENED CRIMINALS ARE NOT TREATED WITH SUCH INDIGNITY.

IT IS MY HOPE THAT ANYONE WHO FEELS THE PAIN BROUGHT ON BY THE EVENTS THAT OCCURRED WITH MY AFFILIATION WITH THE JEHOVAH'S WITNESS ORGANIZATION WILL STOP AND THINK ABOUT WHAT MIND CONTROL DOES TO PEOPLE OR PERHAPS HAS DONE TO THEY THEMSELVES.

TOTAL DOMINATION BY ANY RELIGION LENDS A DISRESPECT, IN MY VIEW, TO THE MIND GOD GAVE US AND ANTICIPATED WE WOULD USE.

THIS IS MY STORY..........

1976

It was dark in the room where my mother had told me to go to bed. I was seven. The adults were playing dominoes in the other room. Going to bed was fine by me. I was so sleepy after a long day of playing with friends at my parents' friends' trailer house. It had been so hot outside.

I had barely closed my eyes, it seemed, when I awoke, gagging. Something was in my mouth, hitting the back of my throat. The smell in my nose was bad, like dirty socks.

"Suck it," I heard. It was the son of my parents' friends. I did what he said. My stomach began to hurt, and the room began to spin. I wasn't sleepy anymore, but was I dreaming? Why would I smell this foulness in my dreams, though? Why would I dream of something so weird?

The light came on. Screaming. Nonstop screaming. It was the boy's mother. My parents came running in. It was a cheap mobile home (not that I knew that then), and it sounded like a stampede on those floors. *Shut up. Please, oh please, just shut up.* I was scared.

When my father jerked me up by my arm, it felt like an Indian burn, when someone takes your flesh between both hands and twists hard. It burned like my flesh was on fire. Dad was angry. The bathroom he took me to in their trailer was also the utility room. He tossed me up onto the washer and dryer like I was a rag doll. The spanking was one of the worst I would ever receive. I had bare legs from playing outside all day in shorts. *Why am I getting a spanking?* I thought. I knew better than to ask that out loud, though. Even as a small child, it was always quite apparent that dads word and action was law. He displayed a great deal of disgust and anger if we disagreed with any decision he made or was making. It was a tiny room, and I scrambled around, trying to escape the next hit. The room seemed to get smaller every second. Then, there was silence. I didn't see the boy or the parents when we left.

Riding home in the back of the station wagon, I watched for lights. I liked the way there would be darkness and then a glimpse of light, which was quickly gone again. Then, streetlights were no more. We lived in the country.

I awoke the next morning with a desperate need to brush my teeth. My mouth tasted funny. Gross. I went into the kitchen. My mother acted like nothing had happened. She was good like that. Many times mom would seem frustrated by any number of things. Yet, she seemed to be adept at just letting things play out. Not one to make a fuss or deal with the unpleasant. She was making breakfast. I didn't want any today. I had a funny feeling in my stomach. They would force me to eat anyway. Mom would be nice about it. She was the type that would offer to make you something else if you didn't like what she was preparing. Dad discouraged that. "Make them eat what you're cooking." She would quietly ask us anyway. Soon, eating would no longer interest me, and she would be particularly concerned. With Dad, though, there wasn't a chance he would display any form of concern that I might be damaged and I knew it. My legs hurt. Maybe it was sunburn, but I don't think so.

When Dad hit you, he hit you hard and many times in a row. It took your breath away. That was the worst part—when I couldn't breathe anymore. With Mother, you had a feeling of unconditional love. Not so with Dad. You had to earn it. Why I sought him out that morning, I don't know. I got dressed and remember going off specifically to find him.

We had twenty acres, but he wouldn't be hard to find. There he was, working outside. Dad was a tall, thin man with dark-rimmed glasses and a big nose. He would sweat when he worked, and his nerdy glasses would slide down. I wondered why that nose didn't hold his glasses up. "Whatcha doin'?" I didn't care what he was doing. No reply. Just silence. He walked away.

Thus, at seven years of age, I got my first dose of shunning. It was Dad's worst—but by no means only—form of discipline.

Why wouldn't he talk to me? I don't even remember what he was doing, but I offered to help. Silence. Eventually, I wandered off. He didn't seem to notice.

I was dirty. From then on, I felt dirty a lot. There was lots of bathing and brushing my teeth. Sometimes, I would bathe three times a day. Scrubbing seemed like a necessity. Only a few hours later, though, I felt the need to bathe again. I would look in the mirror, red from hot water and scrubbing, and my gut reaction was still disgust. *Jesus, what an ugly girl.* It seemed like months but in actuality was probably only a week of being shunned by Dad. Dinnertime was strange during that time. "Can I have some potatoes?" I remember directly addressing him to see if he was inclined to speak to me again. He would look at Mom. She would hand me potatoes. Did I make him sick? Obviously.

Of particular note is what happened a couple of years after this incident. My dad, ever the planner, sat down with his family to inform us of a decision. In the event that something were to happen to Mother or himself, we would be given to their best friends—the parents of the boy who attacked me—and would live with them until adulthood.

This strikes me as horrifying now. At about age nine, it terrorized my daily thoughts. My parents *knew* that abuse had taken place in that home. Why would they arrange for their children to be given to that family? From that moment on, thoughts of my parents dying plagued me.

My mother volunteered to work up on a catwalk at a district convention at a major event center. I sat, shaking inside, trying to crane my neck to see her. "Please, Mom, don't die."

I didn't care much for the new house in Oklahoma. We had moved there from Houston only to get away from what dad would call "worldly life". He wanted to take care of his parents and serve in a congregation that would provide him the opportunity to support the Jehovah's Witnesses to the fullest. I didn't get along with my sister. It was so bad at one point that my dad built a divider into an already small room. Her share was the front part of the room, and she didn't want me to walk through her part to get to mine. Mom encouraged us to just get along for the sake of peace in the house. So daily I would walk through my sisters part of the room to my own. I was always careful not to touch her things. Outside was wonderful, though, with plenty of room to roam. I was usually alone.

Anything that happened before the move to Oklahoma is merely information given to me by my mom over the years. Dad had been an engineer at NASA and was heavily involved in the "race for space." The Russians were trying to put the first man on the moon, and the United States desperately wanted to beat them to it. We lived in Houston, and I was born in 1969. I had one older sister and one younger brother. We weren't Jehovah's Witnesses then, but my mother had been raised around the faith when her mother died. Her father didn't want her, so he gave her to her older brother and his wife to be raised.

Dad had worked long and hard for NASA, rubbing elbows with the astronauts. My mother now openly admits that it was his position that turned her on. She was a secretary for a firm that subcontracted for NASA, and that's how they met. Dad was in the control room when the now famous "Houston, we have a problem" call came in. He was there when Armstrong took his first steps on the moon's surface. Dad was a brilliant man (and, as far as I know, still is). There was an issue with space travel. To navigate on earth one uses a compass. A compass utilizes gravity to determine true north. In space, there is zero gravity. A space compass was what NASA needed. My dad invented the space compass. The model for the first space compass sits on my brother's desk. It's a little metal thing, but I know what it represents, and I have always been in awe of it.

NASA was Dad's life. The recognition that came with his position was something he relished. Not that I knew it at the time. I don't remember ever seeing him before moving to Oklahoma. I do suspect Mom was unhappy there.

One day, Jehovah's Witnesses came to the door while we still lived in Houston, TX. Apparently, Mom was cordial or accepted literature because they kept coming back. My mother smoked cigarettes, but she knew she shouldn't, and she was embarrassed. Sometimes, she wouldn't answer the door. "Now be quiet," she would say (as she relates it) and push us into an inner room of the house so they couldn't see us from the front door. We would just pretend we weren't home.

Mother was beautiful. She was funny and mild and—best of all, I thought—loved her kids beyond words. She didn't have a good childhood in which she was loved, and it was my feeling that she was creating for us what she hadn't had.

She was a stellar parent, actually. She doted on us when we were sick and always had homemade snacks, a clean home, and evenings devoted to time with us. Mother was a very comforting woman to be around.

Elementary school was sheer hell, so often I faked sick to get to stay home with her. I say elementary school was hell because I was a bit of a nerd and I didn't fit in. Children were awful for the most part. Being one of Jehovah's Witnesses did not help. Whether she believed I was sick or not, her manner was the same. "Lay down on the couch, and I'll turn on the television for you." I felt guilty asking her to change the channel for me when I felt fine. The old-fashioned clicking of the dial as she turned to find a show for me is a sound I remember well. It makes me smile. *Stop! It's Gilligan's Island. Ginger is pretty. Life is good. Maybe today they will find a way off the island.* Being home with her—solely her—was great. I loved her so. I *love* her so. Even as we grew up, you could bet Mom would stop by our bedrooms to make sure we didn't need to talk something through with her. I usually didn't have much to say, but I loved knowing she would ask. Dad made no such stops by our doors. If he did, there was to be a whipping involved.

With Mother, you got the feeling she missed you whenever you were away at school. She always eagerly welcomed us home. She didn't seem as eager to see Dad come home. I think it was her unhappiness that drove her to be receptive to Jehovah's Witnesses. Apparently, Dad agreed to meet with them sometime after Mom began visiting with them regularly. Years later, he would say he only agreed to meet with them to prove them wrong. This was to no avail. Finally, he had found the one true religion, he would say. Mother and Dad were baptized in 1975 as Jehovah's Witnesses.

Dad made the decision that his long-worked-for career was impeding his spiritual progress with the Jehovah's Witness organization. He wanted to move his family away from the "rat race." I thought it was funny he had called his career the "space race," and now it was a "rat race."

His parents lived in Oklahoma, so he reasoned it was best to move closer to them and it suited his purposes to get away from the big city life and begin his new spiritual career in a smaller setting. Houston, Texas, to Clayton, Oklahoma, proved to be culture shock for Mother. Clayton was tiny. I can only imagine how Mom felt. Nightlife for my parents had once consisted of nights out at the Playboy Club, beach houses, and notoriety. Clayton was to Mom what a Christmas gift of socks is to a child. Granny and Granddad, my dad's parents, were not thrilled with his newfound faith. I have very clear memories of the first visit to their home after Dad had chosen a career with Jehovah's Witnesses. Dad, Bible in hand, brought us all in and began to witness to them. Livid would be a vast understatement to describe his family's reaction.

We left abruptly. Thereafter, when we would visit, Granny would be lovely but quiet. Granddad, however, would saddle up and ride away. Often, we could see him from the house in the distance, waiting for us to leave. Granny was much like my mother. She just wanted everyone to be happy and worked tirelessly to that end. They lived in a large place in the country—in the middle of nowhere, basically. A river ran right through their front yard, and they built cabins so people could come and rent them and fish. It was a very remote place, and city life was not something they ever wanted to experience. When Dad was being considered for a NASA job, they were extremely proud. Their small-town boy had made good. The FBI had even visited their remote home when doing the background check on Dad. He was big talk in a little town.

The Watchtower Society of Jehovah's Witnesses had heard of Dad's remarkable decision to leave such a high-profile job to further Kingdom interests. They asked him to write his life story, as they wished to publish it in *The Watchtower,* a magazine printed by Jehovah's Witnesses and published worldwide. His story appeared in the May 1, 1982, edition of *The Watchtower* magazine. Instantly, he reached celebrity status among Jehovah's Witnesses. He didn't brag about his accomplishments, but the article was special to him, and rightly so.

I thought it was cool that he didn't brag. Instead, he encouraged his family to play down those accomplishments because they meant nothing when compared with working for God's Kingdom. He felt all his work and education had been "a vanity and a striving after the wind."

He did, however, seem to have a drive to climb the theocratic ladder, as it were. It's not openly spoken of, but within the Jehovah's Witness organization, there is a pecking order. At the bottom are the weak ones. They are the ones with no drive to excel in theocratic pursuits. Dad wasn't one to not excel. We were Wendell's family, and we seemed to rank higher in the chain as Dad quickly became important in the organization.

My brother, sister, and I attended a small rural school. Dad's ever-present concern was our being in public school. We were drilled regularly to have no "worldly friends." We couldn't celebrate holidays anymore, either. Regular study, field ministry, and meeting attendance at the Kingdom Hall were all designed to help us thwart Satan's influence. After all, being in the center of God's one and only true organization on earth would protect us. Those not participating in the three activities vigorously enough were dangerously teetering on destruction. Losers.

"Bullshit" would prove to be an understatement. Dad was smart, though, and all I knew to do was trust every word from him. Not much infuriated and frustrated my father more than for someone to not follow his counsel to the letter. If someone, even an adult, chose to ask for his advice and then didn't follow it, he would have a terribly bitter attitude. If anyone sought his counsel and didn't do "just so," he would decline to offer that person advice again. Well, he would if he or she begged. He responded to others' desperation for his input or help. "Just so" is an expression he harped on. It's a phrase used in the Bible when speaking of Noah's willingness to follow Jehovah's instructions in building the ark. No halfhearted following of advice. No customizing it to fit what suits you or your personal feelings or situation. "Just so" means *just so.*

We attended a small Kingdom Hall, where Dad was quickly feared as much as revered. There was little doubt Dad was smarter than others there—or at least more educated. Book smarts he had. Folks in this congregation were largely farmers with little education, and they seemed intimidated by him. He was the big man on campus, from what I could tell. There was one exception: an older man named Ronnie Lawrence, then the "presiding overseer," a cocky man who obviously ran the show. He had a mousy, petite wife and a son several years older than me. Tommy was wonderful, and I worshiped him. He treated the three of us kids wonderfully. He treated us like we mattered.

Tommy was an impeccable dresser. Ronnie, not so much. He wore those tacky polyester jumpsuits everywhere except for the Kingdom Hall. The jumpsuits were thin and had the awful faux buckles in the front. *Yes, dress those ugly jumpsuits up with a shiny buckle that goes unattached to any belt at all. The socks with your sandals and comb-over gray hair accentuate your look.* Even at age eight, I thought, *What the...*Yet, shockingly, he had a confidence about him. An "enjoy the glance, ladies" kind of confidence. Yuck.

Ronnie liked me almost immediately, but differently than Tommy did. My first impression of him was that he was creepy, but I never really voiced that at first. We were to be respectful and earned spankings—which were to be avoided at all costs—when we weren't.

So when Ronnie asked me to work with him in service (the field ministry), I wasn't thrilled. Mom assured me it would be OK, and I knew better than to put up a fuss. Ronnie usually led the meetings for field service and formed car groups. Car groups were formed to most effectively get "witnessing territory" covered. Typically ones in the congregation would drive vans if they wanted to be considered serious ministry participants. This is because vans would seat eight people. This facilitated getting the most people out into the field ministry. We were not to change the groups he formed. It was considered a sign of lack of submission, especially from sisters or children. If a brother needed to change the groups, he could do so, but not openly. He could speak to Ronnie privately afterward.

I sat next to him in the car, where he instructed me to sit. He filled the car mostly with sisters when he could. It's my feeling that men in his group, without saying a word, challenged him in some way. He wanted absolute authority. Other men intimidated him. That's my educated guess. We were well-equipped little ministers. I was approximately eight years old at this point, but I had a memorized presentation. Still, I was scared to death when people opened their doors. I felt tiny.

Before leaving the Kingdom Hall, we made sure we had stacks of literature to dispense. I had a cheap little book bag stuffed with literature. If I let it get dog-eared, it was a sign of disrespect for the literature "the faithful slave" had dispensed to us as "food at the proper time." The "faithful slave" was defined as any Jehovah's Witness who had the heavenly hope. Specifically, though, the governing body of Jehovah's Witnesses was a small group of "anointed men" who were said to have been entrusted by Christ with the job of dispensing "spiritual food" to the great crowd (those not going to heaven). I would get mad when a tract would get dog-eared and tear it up and throw it away. It seems silly now. Isn't a dog-eared tract better than one in the trash if it proclaims the good news that leads to everlasting life? The harsh bottom line with Jehovah's Witnesses is that they come to your door with the good news that leads to everlasting life. If you accept their teachings and conform to their standards, you will gain life. The heavenly class of 144,000 individuals is considered the only ones to be allowed into heaven. It is filled with righteous Jehovah's Witnesses already. You will fall into the "great crowd" of those who will soon clean up the dead bodies of the wicked and turn earth back into a paradise. Reject them, and you will be one of the bodies. Many times, after being rejected at the door, we would say, "Fine. It's your funeral," as we walked away.

Already a Christian? Sorry. You too will die if you turn Jehovah's Witnesses away. You are no friend of Christ. That's an awful lot of responsibility for an eight-year-old, you say? No shit.

Ronnie also had a leather book bag, but he didn't keep all of his literature in it. He kept a small stack on his lap. It seemed inconvenient to drive with it there. But what better way to hide an impending hard-on than with spiritual food dispensed at the proper time by "Mother," God's earthly organization? "Mother" is a term used by Jehovah's Witnesses to demonstrate affection for their earthly organization.

Ronnie didn't take no for an answer from people at their doors. We all had time and placement reports to fill out monthly, so we kept track of every minute in the field along with placements. We dutifully reported our activity, all we had done for Jehovah. I bet Ronnie had a big, fat time report.

When we first dropped the rest of the group off on a street ripe for them to work door to door, I felt my stomach get sick. On a different street, he slid my little hand under his stack of *The Watchtower* and *Awake!* magazines. He was hard, like the boy when my parents played dominoes. He moaned but seemed so relaxed. I guessed guys just wanted their pee-pees played with. Why did it always have to be me? I didn't realize at first that this little routine would happen many times in the years to come.

I was young and ignorant. I assumed all males had little girls they bothered with this nonsense. He would reward me with an invitation to come swim at his house and spend the night. I begged not to go. My parents consistently responded by telling me I needed to stop being a baby and be respectful. "Go on. It might be fun," they said. *Sure, it will. It'll be fun for him.*

From when I was eight to when I was about thirteen, Ronnie wanted me with him.

At his house, he would put his hand under my bathing suit and mine in his. His wife sat, watching TV when bath time came, and he bathed me thoroughly behind a locked door. There was a small window in that bathroom, but it only overlooked the backyard. The street was where I wanted to run to. I used to think, *If only I could make it to the street.* But where would I go? At eight, you have no real options that you know of, but you can dream. I would daydream of living in a different kind of environment, one with no door-to-door ministry. Maybe I'd even have a Christmas. Until then, I developed a survival skill. I began to be able to mentally just adapt to whatever situation I found myself in.

That skill is what would keep me tolerant of many an upcoming situation. *Smile. Buy something nice for yourself. Dress pretty, and stay thin.* An endless array of coping skills.

He never bothered me at actual bedtime. Thank God for small favors. After he molested me in the bathtub, we would study *The Watchtower* for the following day's meeting, preparing a comment for me. The study of *The Watchtower* always meant reading the paragraphs and then answering the cited questions. Ronnie would help me prepare a comment to these questions and be praised for having taken the time with me to consider spiritual things. *Being careful, though, not to stray from the Society's explanation of the topic.*

My parents seemed proud he had taken me under his wing. I was far less thrilled. Ronnie told me I was the least attractive in my family and that I should be grateful he would pay me that kind of attention.

I have one child. She is beautiful in every way. I cannot, in my wildest nightmare, comprehend the vileness of saying something like that to her. "You are the least attractive of your family, and no one will ever want you in this way."

Children nearly always believe what adults say. They remember what you say. So watch what you say. Period.

I began to have behavioral problems. I was angry. I developed an eating disorder—actually, two. Anorexia and bulimia became my only friends. I started wetting the bed again, and it made Dad mad. Mom would have to wash my sheets every day, so they resorted to putting a loud, plastic fitted sheet on my bed.

Soon, it seemed like I had been labeled somewhat of a rotten apple in an otherwise golden family. The episode from when I was seven had seared my mind, and I felt zero worth. I often daydreamed of wandering off, never to be seen or heard from again.

Being a kid was hard enough, but toss in a pedophile or two and being a Jehovah's Witness—give me a break, please, someone. Anyone.

Our driveway was long. We walked it daily to catch the bus to school. Dread filled me as the bus approached. One girl in particular not only hated me but also hated Jehovah's Witnesses. Apparently, she was being raised by parents who hated Jehovah's Witnesses. Apprehensively, I would get on the bus.

On several occasions, the only seat available was next to this awful girl. She smiled as I cautiously sat next to her. *Leave space between us. Don't crowd her and piss her off.*

Thinking back, she must have set it up that way, with the only vacant spot being next to her.

She drew her feet up to the seat. I scooted to the outer edge of the seat. The kick that came and the fall to the bus floor didn't sting nearly as bad as the embarrassment and struggle to keep hot tears in my eyes. A roar of laughter from the rest of the kids went ignored by the bus driver.

When what had been happening came to my parents' attention, it was discussed at our family Bible study. We had been recipients of persecution for the Lord's sake, not unlike when Christ had been spit on and made fun of. We were supposed to be joyful and proud.

Not long after that, despite being warned to not participate, I colored a turkey for Thanksgiving while at school. Ignorant though it was, I took it home. The spanking made me less ignorant the next time.

The visits to Ronnie's house became a routine—a sickening routine. It would be years before I would report him and meet his other victims. The baths were the worst of it, and I hated the field ministry with him that preceded the visits to his home. Tommy, his son, had long since moved out and seemed to hate Ronnie as much as I did. I often saw and heard Tommy and Ronnie argue. Ronnie seemed to have less emotion but Tommy was different. He often would get into the truck and cry as he spoke harshly of his dad.

One day at school, I made a friend. Her name was Sheila, and I was so excited. I asked my mom if she could come spend the night at our home. "Absolutely not. You know no worldly people are allowed here" was the reply.

My wheels began to turn. What, though, if she attended the Kingdom Hall with us? I could maybe study the Bible with her. I approached my mom with the request. To my surprise, she said OK. A fine idea. The visit with Sheila was wonderful, but she wasn't interested in converting, so my parents quickly put a stop to the friendship.

I wasn't popular in elementary school, to be sure. I had adopted a manly sort of dress and grooming. Badly permed hair, glasses, and nearly everyday overalls completed my look. I don't blame kids for steering clear of me. Even if I had been popular, not a soul was allowed to phone me. Boy or girl, it didn't matter; I would be grilled about the extent of our friendship and warned about the inappropriateness of it.

OK. Ronnie can ram his fingers inside me until I bleed, but Sheila can't call to see if I'm bringing enough Twinkies tomorrow for the both of us. OK, Dad.

I'm not sure why, but I assumed Dad knew what was going on with Ronnie. Perhaps this was because he always seemed to know everything, usually so he could discipline us.

Jehovah's Witnesses are a huge network made up of small congregations worldwide. Word travels like wildfire, especially in a circuit of congregations (usually about fifteen congregations). Even faster does word of a wrongdoing spread in one congregation. In any given town, the town itself is generally oblivious to what's going on with members of Jehovah's Witness congregations. That is because Jehovah's Witnesses live in a vacuum in which there is no socialization with nonmembers. All wrongs get handled internally. No real friendships are to be formed, even with coworkers or schoolmates, because their worldliness will taint you. Even having lunch with these people is the first step to "falling away from the faith." Thus, it is expected you will keep contact to a minimum. This is true even regarding family members who won't accept your faith.

When I was around the age of thirteen, Ronnie lost interest in me. Maybe I missed the attention because I sought it from anyone who would give it. I received counsel around the age of fourteen for hugging too much. The wife of a brother had come to the elders with concerns that my hugs "lasted too long."

At the age of about fifteen, I met a girl at a Kingdom Hall building project. She was older. She was from a congregation about two hours away. She was beautiful with dark, wavy hair. Her upper lip was crooked when she smiled. I was homely, but she was lovely in every way. She was the envy of all young sisters and the object of desire for all young brothers—probably older ones as well.

She liked me. I was funny and could knock her socks off with my Jimmy Carter impersonation. She asked my parents if I could come spend a few weeks with her in the summer when school let out. My dad trusted her parents as spiritual people as they were longtime Jehovah's Witnesses. He let me go. Freedom at last, and no Ronnie hovering, watching.

We participated in the field ministry together as well as meetings, shopping, and laughing. A lot of laughs. She had a boyfriend, but she didn't seem to care. She seldom spoke of him and it almost seemed like she just was entertained by his attentions. I never wanted him around anyway.

One night at her house, I awoke to her hand inside my panties. I rolled over and pretended to be asleep. Night after night, she repeatedly tried, and I always pretended to sleep. I went home and never uttered a word to my parents. This was different than Ronnie. I loved her. My mom and dad would think it filthy.

Despite letter writing, our friendship waned, and I was devastated.

About the age of sixteen, Ronnie's son, Tommy, asked me to help him with his house cleaning jobs. I said yes. I was grateful for anything that got me away from home. The money was good, but his friendship was better.

Tommy was not a manly man, for lack of a better term. He had bleached highlights in his hair, a dark tan, and sparkling white teeth. He was always in fashion. His second marriage was failing. I loved him like a brother.

One day, parked outside a client's home, he said, "Deb, Dad touched you, didn't he?" The look on his face was sad, and he never made eye contact. He looked straight ahead out the windshield of his white pickup truck.

"I don't know what you're talking about, Tommy," I said. With that, he pulled onto the road and explained, straight faced, how Ronnie had insisted Tommy have sex with others while he watched years ago when Tommy was young. Tommy detailed the horrors of his father's abuse. He knew his father to be a perverse man. He told of how his dad watched him have sex with someone, studied *The Watchtower* magazine with him, and finally took him to the meeting at the Kingdom Hall and prayed for the sins of the congregation. I wasn't stunned, really. I knew Ronnie's house to be the dark, scary, perverse place he described. I tried to act cool. He said, "One day you will tell me." Even though I lied to Tommy that day, we were bonded to one another from that point on.

I had always been in awe of Tommy. How could one so much cooler than I treat me like a queen? He was the type of person who would walk on fiery coals to please another person. I later adopted a similar behavior pattern. Tommy was beloved by my mother. They were close and worked a lot of field service hours together. Sisters loved him. It became evident to me, though, that brothers in the congregation avoided him. *Why? Tommy is way cooler than any of you stuffy guys,* I thought.

One day, I secretly opened my dad's briefcase. It held neatly labeled file folders. Tommy's name was on one. I wish I could say his behavior problems that were outlined within were shocking, but it was like reading about what I was becoming. He had admitted fantasizing about men, masturbation, and infidelity. My stomach sank because I had breached the briefcase. It held sacred confidences of the wrongs perpetrated by all the members of the congregation. I felt worse that anyone's perceived wrongs were dutifully noted in a file for elders to peruse and discuss. Hypocritically, I had been taught that God throws one's wrongs so far over his shoulder that he never even calls them to mind again. Why, then, were all the folders of wrongdoings being carried around for elders to check back on at any given time?

I would soon amass my own file. Lovely. It isn't even one of the pretty ones. Seriously, I've seen it. It's old-school tan, not brightly colored. Maybe they would let me BeDazzle it.

On Thursday nights, more times than I can count, I would fall asleep waiting for the elders to finish meeting with someone or about someone in the back room of the Kingdom Hall. Tommy had been dealt with by the elders on many occasions. I had seen him leave the elders' room in tears. Then again, he cried easily. Not me. I'm tough. He always seemed to me to be a man on the edge—never really on an even keel. So when he was disfellowshiped, I wasn't surprised, really.

To Jehovah's Witnesses, being disfellowshiped for wrongdoing is worse than traumatic. It starts with either an admission of guilt (the admission makes the elders' job easier) or a rumor of wrongdoing. Many things constituted "wrongdoing". It could be adultery, immorality, heavy drinking etc. If a rumor gets back to the elders, they will approach you and ask to speak with you privately. If it is true but you prefer to keep it private, you may choose to lie or decline to answer. Should you choose this route, the matter is far from over.

Cases of this type were few and far between in our little congregation. Tommy was put out of the congregation, it was hard. The congregation knows when the announcement is made that all Jehovah's Witnesses everywhere must shun the offender. Ah, fond memories of age seven. When I say "shun," I mean it in the absolute sense. No individual is to utter a word to the offender, even if he or she speaks to that person. It is designed to sadden you to the point of returning to God.

Tommy had two children with his second ex-wife—and a boyfriend.

Homosexuality was, as my dad used to say, "the most disgusting of all demonic perversions." Soon after his ousting from the congregation, Tommy killed himself. I hammered my mother for any scraps of information about him. Everyone was very tight lipped. My dad seemed mostly relieved that he was gone, and I just didn't get it. Why? Tommy was one of the best people I had ever known. He wouldn't just give you the shirt off of his back; he would press it and gift wrap it first. The only tidbit I could get was that his boyfriend had broken it off with him. Devastated, he had swallowed too many pills and went to sleep, never to wake. *Are you fucking kidding? We are going to leave it at that? All right, Mom.* The talk was now focused on his good qualities, and the file in the mysterious, fat briefcase no longer mattered. "Maybe now God will give him a chance to enter paradise. After all, perhaps he was just mentally ill. God will see his heart's condi tion. We just don't know." This was the talk of the congregation. It was devastating news, but I was unable to have talked to him prior to his death. I shunned him for the most part because I still lived at home and had little opportunity to talk with anyone, much less a shunned one.

Somehow, I envied his freedom, though. It was over. According to Jehovah's Witnesses, he surely didn't qualify for heavenly life. He was asleep in his grave, awaiting God's decision as to whether he would be resurrected on paradise earth. Congregants seemed sure Tommy was not of the 144,000 who were destined for heaven. So the alternative hope for after a resurrection was the hope of living forever in a paradise earth. I was sad for his children but happy for him.

Ronnie was still quite a dominant force in the congregation. It was long before the days of caller ID, and I shivered each time the phone rang. Many times, it was Ronnie, phoning Dad to discuss behavior problems in the congregation. His wife even helped him police the young ones in particular. She reported on the teens regularly.

I had changed schools at the beginning of my ninth-grade year. As a stoic anorexic and bulimic, I was bone thin, and that fact bolstered my bravery as I entered a new school. Not a soul could out-thin me. It was one thing I could control.

Mother had taken notice of my frail frame. She was concerned, and rightly so. I felt so weak and dizzy all the time. I'm sure she spoke to Dad about it because one day, when I had passed on dinner again, they sat in front of me at the dining table with a stack of buttered bread, demanding that I eat. I ate. I threw up. Thin felt great. I was about five feet ten all of a sudden and about one hundred pounds. Thin made me feel ready to take on the world. My glasses were gone; I had a new hairdo and a newfound love affair with makeup. I was a far cry from the nerd of elementary school. I hated her. I hated the girl who had walked in from recess to a quiet, still classroom and no teacher. I was once approached by a scrawny kid a head shorter than I. He was the class clown and troublemaker. He was always badly behaved. "Will you be my girlfriend?"

"Well, yes," I said. I was so excited. Me, the dirty nerd.

The class burst into laughter. I had been set up by the badly behaved boy to be made a fool of.

High school brought new worldly associates into my life, as did the new tanning salon my dad purchased for my sister so she could make a living and easily join the ministry full time. At the time, the requirement to be considered full time was ninety hours a month. Open from 7:00 a.m. to midnight, the salon quickly became a hangout for high school kids who were loving the new tanning trend.

Mom and Dad despised the ease of worldly association at the salon, and they tried to quash it where possible by discouraging people from being there unless they were paying customers.

As for me, I took a job bagging groceries as part of my workforce class requirement. It was hard work. To this day, I don't ever ask baggers to carry out my groceries. They need the break.

I met a large black kid at the grocery store. He was maybe eighteen. His name was Robert. We became fast friends and laughed a lot. Making fun of management in their SAS shoes became more hilarious when my mom bought my first pair following a bout of chronic foot pain. The first day I showed up in them, he made fun of me hard, but I didn't mind.

I informed him of my JW life. He knew there would be no after-work cruises around the Sonic, no happy birthdays, no friendship I could tell my parents about. He knew he couldn't call me.

One night, Robert and I were closing the store together. It was bitterly cold and rainy. I could see that my mom, God love her, had pulled up to pick me up. Robert and I walked out, and I opened the door to get in the car. I said, "G'night."

In typical Robert fashion, he turned to me and said, "Merry Christmas!" It was a joke; he knew of our strict no-holiday rule, and further, Christmas was long gone. It was a new year.

Dumb as it was, I replied, "Yeah, Merry Christmas." My mother was silent, but only until I shut the car door. Then came the bitter lecture. What a disappointment I was. How dare I utter those foul words? Did I not remember Christmas is false worship? A pagan celebration.

"Yes, Mom. I remember. I'm sorry."

"Do you believe pagan worship is a joking matter?"

"No, Mom, I sure don't."

I crawled into bed that night, longing to be anywhere but home.

Rhonda was my best friend within the organization. I was jealous that she had a close cousin she seemed to idolize. Her cousin was promiscuous, which intrigued me. Her mother was a devout Jehovah's Witness, but her father was an unfriendly non-JW. The cousin snuck out regularly and had sex with boys in their pickup trucks. It wasn't her sexual activity that intrigued me as much as her arrogance. She was a pretty teenager but not beautiful. Pretty typical, actually. Yet for all of her averageness, she had the cockiness of a beautiful, accomplished woman. To this day, she is that way. Average looks, average height, average intelligence. She looks down her nose at others, is very much a slacker in the Jehovah's Witness world. I say slacker because she misses a lot of meetings, never comments or visits much with the rest of the congregation. She is vastly overweight, but she seems to take delight in looking down her average nose at others. It is beyond me how this ever happens. On my best day, I feel like an inferior being. Go figure.

My first attempt at sneaking out was with Rhonda. I say "attempt" because it was an epic failure. Getting outside the house was easy. Mom was gullible, and Dad was oblivious until after the fact. Not getting caught proved much harder for Rhonda and me. We crept out and waited to see the headlights from her boyfriend's pickup. When we saw them, we ran toward the road. It was my sister coming home from work. It's laughable now, but it definitely wasn't then. It was chaos. Dad took the door to my room off its hinges. In hindsight, I don't blame him for that. I was already planning my next venture out. Now, screwing my windows shut—that was a little extreme. I would never go out the window. It would muss my hair.

At the next meeting, Ronnie asked to speak with me. He reprimanded me for my actions and wanted to know if I had been having sex. Every time thereafter that I got into trouble, he wanted to know had I been having sex. If so, had I had an orgasm? Was there penetration or just making out? If there was fondling, where was it, and did I enjoy it?

Not surprisingly, he became more and more disgusting over the years. The ease with which he reprimanded people in the congregation was amazing to me. If a baby was crying and disrupting the meeting, he would simply rise from his seat, take the child from its parents, and go outside to whip him or her.

Years later, a directive from the organization addressed the whipping of children outside at the Kingdom Hall. There were to be no more whippings outside, where passersby might see and not understand. Now, most Kingdom Halls have "mother's rooms." These are used for the whipping of unruly children.

I found it increasingly difficult to attend the Kingdom Hall with Ronnie. He would give talks from the platform and pray on behalf of the congregation. When we had group *Watchtower* study, he would comment on the evils of immorality. Hypocrisy is preached against heavily in the organization, but is all too often a way of life.

By my senior year in high school, I was so plagued by anxiety, I began to have panic attacks. Anxiety surfaced from seemingly nowhere. My weight was a constant concern and the feeling of just not measuring up plagued me constantly. Meeting at the Kingdom Hall for the field ministry made me nauseous but was required for all Witnesses. *Otherwise, you're not a Witness, now, are you?*

I graduated high school in 1987. I had a friend, Monte, who took a liking to my sister. She wasn't interested, but it wasn't because he was worldly. She strung along plenty of the worldly boys. When she rebuffed him, he set his sights on me. We had fun, but sex with him did not interest me in the least, and I adamantly said no.

About this time, I decided to move out of my parents' home. A local chiropractor had given me a full-time job. I phoned Rhonda from there to tell her my plan. Within the hour, I walked into my house and was confronted by my mother and my brother. Mother told me to get my things and get out. My friend had called and, "concerned for my spiritual welfare," spilled the beans. I was surprised she had betrayed me. She had frequently trespassed the organization's rules herself. She would bounce right back from her rebellions, though, claiming to be strongly spiritual. After a transgression, she would comment even more at meetings and be more active in the field ministry. Bouncing from good to bad behavior is common among young adult Jehovah's Witnesses. My family was used to my bouncing, so I was accustomed to the looks on their faces as I left. Disgust. My brother told my mom not to waste time on me and that I would soon die at Armageddon.

I called Monte to come get me, and he came right away. He helped me find an apartment that was walking distance from work. My parents had kept my car. I didn't even care. I would've walked away. I knew that keeping my car was a way for my parents to make my life even harder, thus bringing me running back quicker.

Leaving my little basement apartment one morning for work, I noticed him: Ronnie, sitting across the street, watching my apartment. I felt nauseous and scared. He called out as I passed his car, "Had sex yet?"

I yelled no and kept walking. My anger at him was really rage—the kind of rage that makes you cry and then be mad at yourself for crying. I fantasized about his death. Time marched on, but he didn't seem any closer to death.

I liked Monte, but it wasn't the kind of like that became real love—the kind that leads to marriage and kids, the kind I should've felt. Repeated attempts by him led to sex, though. I don't know if I could even consider it my first time, and I still don't. It was absolutely awful. He did his thing and, without a word, got up and went into the other room to watch television. As I lay there crying, the phone rang. It was Ronnie. It was as if he knew. "Yes, I did it," I said.

Now, as an adult, I find it laughable as much as disturbing that I had every right to not talk with him about what had happened and yet did not consider silence. Knowledge of one's wrongs, I feel, is known by God. That is enough. How unfortunate that Jehovah's Witnesses worldwide believe sins must be reported to an elder to be forgiven. Whether a supposed wrongdoer was willing or unwilling to comply with an investigation, elders are on the case. Rumors of wrongdoing stir them up, and they will find out. They will wear you down. It is their claim that these tactics serve to protect and keep God's organization pure. I want to scream at my young adult self, "Keep your mouth shut!" "Yes, I did it" came out without hesitation.

"We will need to meet with you about it."

"I know."

Within the Witness organization, when wrongdoing is admitted, a judicial committee is formed. Ronnie was the chairman of my judicial committee, which also consisted of his aging father and one other brother, Austin. My dad called him Austin-tatious because he bragged a lot.

I was eighteen, and my parents were already shunning me, despite no formal disfellowshiping as of yet. Opposite me at the judicial table sat the three men, grilling me on what sex was like for me. I answered the best I could. Ronnie was angry; the other two were just disgusted.

I told them I was sorry, and they read me scriptures that applied to "my situation." For example 1 Corinthians the 5th chapter deals with sins of an immoral nature. I found it odd Ronnie could stomach himself. I know I could not.

Disfellowshiping means a total loss of all you hold dear. Family, gone. Friends, gone. Support, gone. The key to what action is taken against you is supposed to be how repentant you seem. Of course I was repentant. Sex with men seemed gross to me. Men seemed to only use females. I wanted to say, "I've got your number, moron," to every man who ever came on to me. I never did. I was nice. Always nice. Even when it was to my own detriment.

The elders dismissed me to discuss my fate. Ronnie called me back in. He said, "If you will marry the boy, we might see fit to let you stay in the congregation." No way. Why did I have to marry him to prove my repentance? He wasn't even a JW.

It soon became apparent to me that the brothers in charge, including my dad, wanted to marry me off. Perhaps some man could tame my wildness.

Fool that I was, I answered the door when Ronnie came to my house. "You're obviously not repentant, and we've decided to disfellowship. I'm going to put you out and keep you out."

It didn't make sense. Monte was not a Witness, so marrying him in itself was considered a sin. It was the disobedience to Ronnie's suggestion that made him pissed off. I had cowered many a time to him. I wasn't in the mood anymore.

He explained that if I wanted to try getting reinstated, I could write a letter and formally request it. At that point, the elders would outline the steps for me to get back in. Nice and hard steps.

Let me just say here that being ousted from the organization by the man who had molested me was a surreal experience. To have a piece of shit sit in judgment of my wrongs made me dizzy. But the thought of having to request reinstatement from the same piece of shit was too much to bear. It created in me a rebel that scared even me.

You know that feeling when you first get a haircut or a new pair of jeans? It's that "look out, world; I'm coming out" kind of feeling. That was me. Cocky. Full of myself. My mother came to see me before the announcement was made. She was angry. I was too. "Amazing that the man who molested me for years can disfellowship me and take away my family!" The words just flew out.

She yelled at me to not disrespect that man of God. "Shut your lying mouth!" She didn't seem too worried that she was about to be completely cut off from me. Inside, I shook with fear at the thought of it. She seemed done with me. I had embarrassed them. Again.

All righty.

The months that followed were fun. I didn't party much. I never did drugs, and I didn't drink too much. I just lived what felt like a normal life. I missed my mother badly but not really anyone else.

Monte asked me to marry him. Sort of. I was sitting in the backseat, and his friend was sitting in the front. He went into a store, came out, and threw a box containing a ring into the backseat. It didn't feel anywhere close to the right thing, but I felt safe with him. We were married. All the while, my thoughts would occasionally drift to an imaginary female—maybe one who would hold my hand or lay down next to me at night. *God, I'm gross,* I thought.

Eventually, I left the chiropractor's office where I worked. He and I didn't see eye to eye. He was a former marine, and I was very much a Jehovah's Witness at heart. The deal breaker was when he asked me to ride on a float in an armed forces parade downtown. Declining, I stated my conviction—or, at least, what I had been taught—that all war or support of it was wrong and any who fought or supported our troops would soon be destroyed at Armageddon. I certainly didn't want to be seen on a float in a parade with him. It would ruin my chances of getting reinstated.

The doctor was furious. The next morning, it was raining. He came into the office and told me to clean his shoes. I said that of course I would. "Please hand them to me, and I'll take them into the back."

He smiled devilishly. "Clean them on my feet."

"Do you need two weeks' notice?"

"Nope."

And that was that.

The unemployment office sent me to work at a local restaurant as a hostess. I was living in two different cities and trying to make the commute work. I loved it. Home life was not an issue. Nobody seemed to care where I was or what I was doing. Monte and I were married but no longer really a couple. I spent a lot of time at the restaurant. It was constantly busy, and I enjoyed meeting new people. One of those people was a man who dropped in to eat, gave me his card, and asked me to call him if I was interested in modeling. I called him and went to work.

Turns out, I was decent at it. I was tall and skinny, though not the best looking. At one job, the man said, "You are not pretty, but you are different, and I want someone who doesn't look like everyone else. You're it."

Modeling is absolutely not what girls think. It is probably the worst possible thing for one's self-esteem. Lucky for me, I didn't have any anyway.

I had no self-esteem, but I had courage. Witnesses would say it was stupidity. Either way, I wasn't scared to try. I wasn't scared to not eat. Days would pass with little more than a cracker or two and a little vodka as a treat. The taste of a fork in my mouth eventually was nauseating. I had long since stopped telling Monte where I was or what I was doing, and he certainly didn't care. Going out of town to see gay friends was an easy out for me. I had met many in the gay community while working in Texas and I liked them. The problem was, whenever I was back in a "normal" setting, I felt choked. It was an indescribable suffocating feeling that I just didn't belong where I was.

Through mutual friends, I came in contact with a girl I had known previously but had lost touch with. We began seeing one another, and by seeing one another, I mean an all-out romance. Nothing felt more normal or correct, and yet the guilt was overwhelming.

A gay community somewhat adopted me. They felt sorry for me, I think. At the time, the party life didn't suit me much. I was skinny—horribly so—and I always felt sick and weak. I wanted my mom.

One day, at my wit's end, I wrote a letter to the Kingdom Hall requesting reinstatement. A week later, Ronnie phoned me. Damn, I had hoped he would be dead. He outlined the steps required to be reinstated and get my family back.

Among them: make all meetings at the Kingdom Hall. Sit in the back row and attempt to speak to no one. I would be shunned about six months to a year longer. Suffering this process would somehow demonstrate humility. *When would Ronnie know humility?* I wondered.

I had spoken often of him to my recently acquired friends, and we would jokingly ponder ways to speed his demise. Later, I would have a dear friend who would suggest antifreeze in Jell-O. Oh, but how to get him to eat the Jell-O. Hurting him physically would never happen, though. I would come to know a lot of people the world would benefit from losing. It isn't our place to remove them.

I decided, resolutely, that being gay was not for me, but neither was life with Monte. I would live a straight life and be a model Jehovah's Witness.

It would be hilarious, I think, but also sad and mortifying for one to watch in time lapse the time period of proving repentance. Once it commences for any poor prodigal Jehovah's Witness, it needs to be set to time-lapse video and distributed by some means of viewing by the masses. Walk in the Kingdom Hall alone. Attempt no contact with anyone. Pay rapt attention to the meeting; the elders are watching.

Sit toward the back. Observe the family you have been alienated from as they mingle, laughing with others as they pretend not to notice you. During the final song of the evening, make an exit so the general godly ones aren't inconvenienced by encountering you after the meeting.

If you want new literature, request it from the pedophile who ousted you. Do not ask the literature servant, who shouldn't have to make eye contact with you.

At the time, this disgusting ritual was repeated about three times a week. I had a job that interfered with one of the weekly meetings. I received a phone call from Ronnie informing me my repentance couldn't be proved. Why? Because I wasn't attending all meetings.

I explained that work interfered. The response: "Then you're putting work before God himself."

Do you put God first when you bring kids to your home with the intent of pleasuring yourself with them, you sick fuck? was what I wanted to say. Instead, I said, "Yes, I understand. I'll do better." I asked my employer for the time off to make the extra meetings I had been missing.

I was nervous the night Ronnie made my reinstatement announcement from the stage. I had met with the elders and begged forgiveness. They had prayed and deemed me worthy of being let back in to associate with other Witnesses freely. However, even after a reinstatement, others are urged to be cautious about their association with newly reinstated members. After all, the world has rubbed off on them. Satan has had them, and the world's foulness is on them.

I got dressed up. Happily marching into the Kingdom Hall, I took my seat alone in the back row. My last day of shunning was almost over. I had survived it.

"This is to inform the congregation that Debbie has been reinstated into the Christian congregation." Many were excited to welcome me back, not the least of whom was my dear mother. How I missed her! There were hugs and tears aplenty.

I glanced around for Dad. He was nowhere to be seen. As the commotion died down, I walked to my car but paused to say thank you to a sister welcoming me back to the fold. It surprised me when Dad strolled by me with his important-man briefcase, got in his car, and drove away without a word to me.

But why? Had I not done all this work for God to forgive me? Had I neglected a step?

I went home and phoned my parents. I could do that now as a reinstated individual. Shunning was lifted.

"What is it, Debbie?" Mom asked. It was late.

"Mom, Dad wouldn't speak to me at the Kingdom Hall earlier."

"I'm aware, Debbie. He feels you owe him a personal apology."

Oh, that's right. He is above God, and I'd forgotten. I dared not speak that out loud. Sarcasm was not to be used in the congregation. The organization has since boldly stated that in print. The governing body feels sarcasm has no place among Christians. Pedophiles? OK, sure. No room, though, for the sarcastic.

I had come this far and figured I might as well go all the way. I entered their home the following morning far different from the cocky person who had left the organization. I felt two inches tall. "Dad, I'm so sorry for what I did and for embarrassing you."

With that, he began speaking to me again. I felt seven years old again.

Dare I tell them I left a devastated girlfriend in Dallas when I walked away? Nope. Not today. *I'm going to be a badass Jehovah's Witness.* That proved difficult.

Monte and I divorced and eventually regained somewhat of a friendship. I went to work for a Jehovah's Witness elder, cleaning carpets and fixing water damage. It was hard work, but I got to work with my brother. We had made amends. We had apologized for unkind words spoken. He was a kind soul with anxiety similar to mine.

We became friends. He was an elder. With that in mind, I asked him one day, "Greg, if there's something I didn't confess when I was reinstated, does it void my forgiveness?"

He promised to get back to me, and he did. "Move on with your life, Deb" was his answer. He went on to explain that if I had asked for forgiveness, God had granted it. I hadn't. It didn't make sense to me anyway. It didn't jive with what Jehovah's Witnesses always taught. One was to confess his or her sin to the older men, who would decide if he or she was repentant enough. Many times, a well-hidden sin, once confessed, was proof enough you were repentant. Elders seemed impressed if a sinner who had a long hidden sin, came forward to confess it without being pressured to do so by any outside source. It was a scary, gross process.

My liking girls wasn't so hidden. The day I left Monte, he yelled at me, "You're gay, aren't you?"

Don't ask me questions you aren't ready to hear the answer to. My appearance alone could've and should've given it away. Man's haircut. Tie, slacks, suspenders. I had virtually no breasts at all. Virtually no fat on my body anywhere. I realized later with the help of a sweet, well-meaning counselor that I had in fact enjoyed losing my breasts. The more manly I looked, the less men would look at me. Perfectly reasonable conclusion.

I took a job doing maintenance at an AT&T building. I was lonely but determined to be as normal as all the pretty little girls flitting about town.

It wasn't long before I met a guy there. Chuck. He was sad all the time, and I was too. Why I didn't just work on myself, I'm not sure. Why did I always feel the need to fix people and help make them all better when I was broken?

It never occurred to me to date girls. Choices in my town were slim, and I wanted to be the perfect Jehovah's

Witness anyway. It didn't occur to me to date Witness men, either. They were better than me. Dating Witness men would've been acceptable. Dating a "worldly person" brought counseling but wasn't a disfellowshipping offense in itself.

My mother asked me who this Chuck person was. I answered, "It's nobody, Mom. If he would go away, that would suit me fine." I meant it. If Chuck had just disappeared I would have been fine. Chuck had emotional issues and instead of working on my own, I tried to help him. It was a losing battle but I kept on.

I wanted to settle down, though, and more than anything, I wanted a child. It was not a storybook romance with Chuck by any means. In fact, we were fire and gasoline from the start. Despite this, we hadn't known each other long when we decided our wants in life were similar. We decided to marry and build a home.

I cheated on him almost immediately. I simply didn't feel a connection to him. I had discussed with him my leaning toward homosexuality, and he seemed unconcerned. He said it was "kind of sexy."

It isn't as if we never got along. We did. The choking feeling was there, though, almost from the start. Suffocation. One night, I awoke in a panic. The room felt so small. I went to the car. "Come back in. This will all be OK," Chuck said as he followed me out. I wanted so badly for that to be true. We had built a nice home. For a typical girl, it would've been so much more than enough. Why couldn't I just be a normal girl? Rhetorical questions. In my case, no answers made a difference anyway—at least, not the ones I kept getting from Jehovah's Witnesses.

The moment I knew I was pregnant, I was ecstatic. Hormonal changes, though, dredged up a myriad of feelings. Anxiety was horrible, and honestly, I considered suicide. During the third trimester, though, my anxiety subsided, and I looked forward to the birth.

One day, the brother I worked for, Bob, for called me into his home. Another sister I knew well, Cissy, was sitting there with her husband. "Have a seat, Deb." Nausea set in, and I had no reason for it yet.

Bob began, "Deb, we all have something in common. We have all been a victim of Ronnie." *No, no, no…I can't do this.* "Did Ronnie touch you as a child, Deb? It's time to come forward."

"Yes. He touched me. He did more than touch me." I was terrified but somewhat backed into a corner. The people gathered here knew and were probably going to tell it whether I did or not. I would likely be dragged into it. So I complied. Bob went on to claim that Ronnie had fondled and propositioned him at the lake while taking a break from the field ministry. Cissy had a far more horrific story, much like my own. Cissy was a pretty girl, and it was no secret that she had been troubled for much of her life. To this day, she has a beautifully kind personality but will tell you she suffers from her memories.

What followed was chaos—months and months of it.

I wanted to just be normal! I wanted to be a good wife, prepare to be a good mom, attend my meetings, and be left alone. Like one of those cans with those stupid toy snakes in them, this wasn't going to be tucked away again without a lot of work.

The elders began to interview us and also seemed to see the light about a lot of troubles from years past. A lot of things were now beginning to make sense. Children's fear of Ronnie, behavior problems that had long been exhibited. All pieces of a growing puzzle.

Ronnie denied the wrongdoing—the crimes—at first. Nonetheless, he stepped down from his prominent position of oversight. He was revered in his status in our congregation. He stated "he was no longer blameless and free of reproach." Good riddance, asshole.

Cissy had come forward years ago but had been disregarded. One key reason why was the Jehovah's Witness Two Witness Rule. If an admission of guilt is absent, there must be two corroborating witnesses to the wrongdoing before the accusation will hold weight with a judicial committee. Now, there were more than two, and one of them was me, Wendell's daughter.

Looking back, I'm not sure why I never contemplated whether Ronnie had harmed others. I had never been a self-absorbed person. I certainly had been no angel, but I genuinely cared for others, especially the underdog.

A judicial committee was formed based on our testimonies, and the confrontations began. Individually, the victims were required to face Ronnie with their accusations. Every person possibly connected was interviewed. My parents were suddenly very supportive calling often to check on me and spending time with me but I increasingly missed my girlfriend, who had always been there in a crisis. She had always wanted to be a parent, and I was about to give birth. She would be excited.

One evening, Chuck and I were going door to door in the ministry, and I said to him, "Chuck, I'm struggling with this homosexuality deal." He said nothing.

I didn't return her calls.

On more than a couple of occasions, I inquired about notifying the authorities of the molestations. The elders assured me that they had been notified and law enforcement had declined to take an interest. For years to come, I fully accepted their explanation. After all, years had passed. Honestly, as a Witness, you get used to disappointment. Your desires are wrong. Your wants are temporary and unnecessary. Paradise will soon come, and then all your wants and desires can be fulfilled. Until then, listen, obey, and be blessed. There is a Kingdom song (songs written only for use by Witnesses at their gatherings) titled exactly that.

As far as Jehovah's Witnesses are concerned, if something of an unpleasant nature arises, it will be handled first and foremost by God's appointed men in God's organization. God's court and his judicial system trump worldly man's court.

I knew that throughout all the judicial proceedings, notes—thorough notes—were kept. All cases get their own file to be preserved forever. Your past is never your past with JWs. It follows you in the form of a file that holds all of your deeds and misdeeds.

Additionally, I knew that there had been ongoing correspondence with the Watchtower Society at their New York office. We, the victims, were not allowed to see the correspondence. We were even instructed not to discuss things among ourselves. Only with our spouses should we talk things through. Forget that.

I wasn't going to pour my heart out to a man who said nothing when I admitted struggling with homosexual urges.

Though Ronnie maintained innocence throughout the majority of the judicial meetings, there was one moment I considered a breakthrough. Exhausted, I yelled at him, "I know why Tommy killed himself!" Ronnie dropped his head to the table and never looked me in the eye again.

After Tommy killed himself, my brother Greg had gone to Tommy's home with Ronnie. Greg witnessed Ronnie pick up a note from close to where Tommy was found, read it, and stick it in his pocket. The note was never given to authorities or anyone else, to my knowledge. It would have been just like Tommy to tell all, though, in a note at the end of his life. He was dramatic like that.

By the last of the judicial meetings, Ronnie knew that I was aware of his sins with his own son.

A judicial committee elder called me. "We are disfellowshiping him, Debbie." I thought it would sound sweeter than it did. Something was terribly lacking. Oh, yes. Prosecution. Prison. I wanted him to suffer fear, humiliation, and physical pain as I and countless other victims had.

Within days, Ronnie appealed the committee's decision. When this happens within the organization, an entirely new panel of brothers is selected from a neighboring congregation to hear the case. These brothers travel to hear the exact same testimonies and arguments. I implored one of them, "Please, don't make me do this again." He dismissed my request and called me to the back room.

We used to call it "getting called in on the back carpet." I don't know why we joked about it because it was anything but funny when it was happening to you. Although it was supposed to be a loving reproof when you got called into the back room by elders, usually for wrongdoing with the goal in mind of bringing the wrongdoer to his senses, it was seldom that in my experience.

The Jehovah's Witnesses organization is based on fear and dominated by men. Leaders believe women "only use a portion of their brains." Thus, they should be grateful for their God-assigned subservience.

There were more victims than just Cissy and I. Boys, girls, men, and women alike made a steady stream of complainants coming forward for the second grilling of Ronnie.

The decision of the appeals committee was unanimous. Ronnie had been found guilty in God's court but was still somewhat arrogant about it. He was always an arrogant man. When I was small, he would admit to me that yes, he had problems, but just like David of the Bible, who slept with Bathsheba and even murdered her husband, he was still used by God as King of Israel. Ronnie never wavered in his belief that he was God's mouthpiece on earth, used by God to bring others to the only true organization.

On Sundays, Jehovah's Witnesses hold a public talk followed by a study of *The Watchtower* magazine. Audience participation is expected. Those who don't participate are considered weak spiritually. All of my life, I watched Ronnie arrogantly express his fucking ignorance at these studies. He had a way of raising his hand that was different from anyone else's. Even my parents laughed at the way he did it. Most would raise their whole arm. As a child, if I didn't fully raise my arm, my mother would reach around me and force it up high. Ronnie, though, would slightly raise only two fingers from the armrest of his seat. It was as if *The Watchtower* study conductor should have been watching anxiously for Ronnie's attempt to comment. If the conductor saw it, he called on him almost without exception. If he missed it, the look on Ronnie's face was priceless. He was furious that he had been overlooked and another comment had been heard. He had a silly little way of laughing at others' comments—a little smirk that suggested it just wasn't quite right. Funny, the things we remember.

The announcement of Ronnie's disfellowshiping was made at the Kingdom Hall. One sister ran from the Kingdom Hall, crying. Oh, dear God, people. This was the same sister who had always rallied behind all the elders' decisions in the past when it came to ousting ones from the congregation. "Must've had a good reason," she would say. But this was a huge deal. Ronnie was a fallen angel in many people's eyes. Yes, that night was a sad night for all who loved him. It was also sad for all of us who really knew what he was because not everyone put stock in what we had to say. Even those who believed it just wanted us to forgive and forget. Even an elder from his committee said, "Debbie, just let this go."

I asked him if he would have just let it go had it been his little girl. The sad answer, despite his silence, was probably yes, he would.

I decided, to the disappointment of my husband and my parents ithat I needed to seek counseling. At the time, the organization somewhat looked down on seeking counseling from outside. The elders and mature ones inside the organization were to be sought in the event one could not handle the stresses of life. This was worse than simple stresses of life. To keep it quiet, I found a counselor about an hour away. She was an excellent human being, by my estimation, and I liked her methods. I shared with her my marital unhappiness. I shared with her the abuse. However, one day, she suggested an idea that didn't sit well with me. "Have you ever considered living a life free of that religious organization?"

Oh my God! How dare she! That religion is the one and only true religion. That organization has my loyalty, albeit having been the most difficult to give my loyalty to. I dismissed her suggestion as foolishness and even bragged to my friends in the congregation that I had quit using the services of a counselor because I had seen the light. Worldly counselors would just try to get you to leave God's organization. I counted myself lucky. I was proud of myself.

I never returned to her. I wish I had.

Soon after, the dust settled, and my beautiful baby girl, Marley, was born. I was in love with her—a vibrant redhead with a fiery personality to match. However, I was unhappy with my decision to marry Chuck. I struggled with attractions to women but certainly didn't want to embarrass my dad or anyone else in my family again. I don't know why Dad's possible embarrassment concerned me. His arrogance embarrassed me.

In the months following Ronnie's ousting, I would hear snippets of conversations about Ronnie having already applied for reinstatement numerous times. I sighed with relief with the knowledge they were not considering it.

Meetings were still hard because, although he was shunned, he attended every one. The elders became aware that he was even holding meetings for field service in his home with certain ones still loyal to him. This was surreal. Under normal circumstances (such as my own ousting), a shunned one tucks his or her tail between his or her legs. It's common to sneak into meetings after they begin and duck out just before they end completely. Not Ronnie, though.

Two years flew by. My dad called me. They were going to reinstate Ronnie. I was furious. Two years of shunning. That's all our innocence was worth?

The elders made a deal with him. "Tell us all the names of the victims so we can shepherd them, and we will allow you back in." In addition, he was to write letters of apology to all his victims. For years, I carried that letter tucked into my wallet behind my driver's license. I eventually became enraged by his handwriting, though, and I destroyed it one day. I didn't know that years down the road, I would get a copy of it again.

Below is a copy.

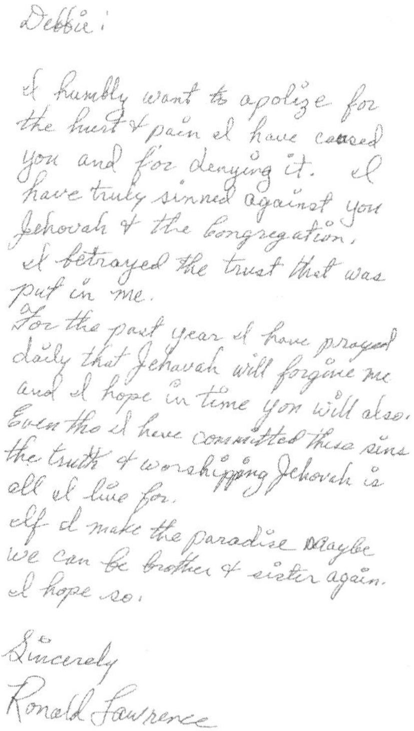

Debbie:

I humbly want to apolize for the hurt & pain I have caused you and for denying it. I have truly sinned against you Jehovah & the congregation. I betrayed the trust that was put in me.
For the past year I have prayed daily that Jehavah will forgive me and I hope in time you will also. Even tho I have committed these sins the truth & worshipping Jehovah is all I live for.
If I make the paradise maybe we can be brother & sister again. I hope so.

Sincerely
Ronald Lawrence

It was done. "This is to inform the congregation that Ronnie has been reinstated into the Christian congregation."

He was swarmed with well-wishers afterward. I took Marley and went to the car. It sickened me to think that she would even know his name as she grew up.

Weeks later, Ronnie tried to speak to Marley—well, not tried, *did.* I blew my top. I went outside the Kingdom Hall with her and screamed. My mother followed me out. "If he ever fucking speaks to my child again, I will start screaming in the middle of the Kingdom Hall," I said. Elders came out and encouraged me to "get a hold of myself."

In the meantime, the elders met with Ronnie. They encouraged him to consider attending a different Kingdom Hall about forty-five minutes away. They told him it was very difficult for victims to have to see him often at the Kingdom Hall.

What plagued me was that the congregation 45 minutes away was filled with children. I suspect I didn't think about other children previously because I wasn't a parent. Now the thought grieved me constantly. He agreed to attend the other nearby Kingdom Hall.

I still saw him routinely around town. On one such occasion, I saw him at a local elementary school as I drove past. I parked and watched him. A little girl I recognized from our congregation ran out of the school and got into the car with him. I followed him. He dropped her off at her home, and I waited for him to leave. I phoned her mother, Marcia, and asked if I could come visit for a few moments, my heart racing. When I arrived at her front door, I never had a moment's hesitation. The whole story spilled out to her as I watched the fury rise in her face. Marcia was new to our area and was not familiar with these facts as of yet. She thanked me for my time, and I left.

Hours later, I was surprised by a phone call from an elder. A meeting with me was requested. God, how sick of these meetings I was becoming. I agreed to meet, knowing I had done nothing wrong. The meeting's objective? To reprove me for sharing "confidential matters" with others who had no right to such knowledge. "Debbie, you're pretty enough on the outside, but your insides could use some work if you don't see the need to keep this Ronnie matter quiet." *Confidential matters? Protect a pedophile before we speak out to protect the children here?*

Marcia had called the elders after my visit. It was never her intent to get me in trouble. She was furious, though, that she had a family that included four small children and yet had never been informed of the danger that lurked.

I was warned that if I couldn't keep my mouth shut, I would be subject to stronger measures. Disfellowshiping. Fuck my life.

Marley was little, and concerns about her safety consumed my thoughts. Some days were worse than others, and knowing Ronnie was once again a happy member of the congregation and in good standing with the organization made me sick.

Although Dad wasn't supposed to share details with me, he gave me tidbits of information about Ronnie. The news was that there were other victims coming forward. Ronnie had vowed to the elders that he had revealed all victims' names. My head was spinning. I trusted no man, anywhere, anytime. We lived in the country and had ATVs. Marley was quite small when Chuck began taking her for short little rides on them around our property. Inside, I would panic. He wouldn't molest her, would he? I would watch them from the window for as long as I could see them. Once they were out of sight, I would panic. I was in a state of upset until I could see them returning home.

Looking back, I know Chuck would choose death over sexually abusing our daughter. In the moment, though, it felt perfectly rational to wonder.

Dad called to tell me Ronnie was being put out of the organization once again, this time for lying. The elders would be "shepherding the newly revealed victims." No talk was focused on informing the authorities.

Jehovah's Witnesses view all authorities as being in only temporary positions. They eagerly await the time when all wicked ones will be destroyed. All government will fall worldwide, and a new world inhabited only by Jehovah's Witnesses will prevail. I often silently questioned why they so readily called on the authorities for protection and order. They didn't do this with the pedophile situation, though. The damage was done and couldn't be reversed, so secrecy was now important. Clean up the mess, and sweep it under the proverbial rug.

One friend of my dad's was a circuit overseer (a traveling overseer dispatched from the Society to check up on and bolster the faith of the congregations). He visited the McAlester congregation when the Ronnie situation was being handled. The McAlester congregation had built, with volunteer labor, an apartment for the circuit overseer across the parking lot from the Kingdom Hall. It made it convenient for the circuit overseer to stroll over for meetings. He strolled over a lot for meetings dealing with Ronnie. He told my dad, "Let's get this guy out and keep him out."

I'm sure the elders hoped Ronnie would just die or disappear when they took action against him the second time. The issue had become the talk of the circuit and beyond. Jehovah's Witnesses are a close-knit, silent-when-necessary community. None of us spoke to worldly ones about this embarrassing matter.

This time, Ronnie was out longer—much longer. He persisted in meeting attendance and coming to circuit assemblies and district conventions. Running into him was a common occurrence. Just because he was disfellowshipped didn't preclude him from attendance at spiritual gatherings, although not a soul could speak to him. He certainly wouldn't have been invited to any social gathering.

Anger would rise up inside me. I daydreamed of ramming a wooden spoon into him as he had those of us with young vaginas. I wondered if it had scared him when I seeped blood into the bathwater the first time he used a wooden spoon on me. It would scare me, were I a pedophile.

I anticipated never actually having to hear his voice again. Being shunned, he wasn't allowed to comment at meetings or speak to anyone. The only exception was if he wanted to speak to an elder about the possibility of reinstatement.

He requested reinstatement regularly, even going above the heads of local elders to the circuit overseer. When that failed, he contacted the branch office of Jehovah's Witnesses, pleading for an act of mercy that would allow him back into the fold.

Local elders complained about his persistence, but still no law enforcement was advised of Ronnie's proven pedophilia.

Several years passed. After years of insistence and assurance from the elders that they would keep Ronnie out, he was once again reinstated. I complained vigorously and am quite sure the elders tired of me just as they had of him.

One day, we had a setup/cleanup day in anticipation of a circuit assembly at the local Expo center. At the time, we held two such events a year. All congregations in our circuit were invited, along with, of course, the public and any interested Bible students. Bible students are any who accept an offer of a home bible study from Jehovah's Witnesses and express a desire to progress toward baptism.

My mother always provided snacks and coffee for the morning of the setup day. I worked until noon daily, so I would drop Marley off with my mother, and she would roam about the large facility, helping where she could. I would join later in the day. As I entered about lunchtime, I was happy to see everyone. It was always a time of catching up with neighboring congregations and good friends. It was bustling with activity. Jobs included setting up the stage, arranging flowers, and even cleaning chairs. The general cleanup by worldly people from any previous event wasn't enough for us, God's chosen, the cleanest of people. Granted, we had a pedophile in our midst, but ousting him had been punishment enough, apparently, and now he was back, repentant.

I went to help scrape gum from the bottom of chairs. There he was. I was instantly nauseous, like all other times I laid eyes on him. He was cleaning windows alongside children and adults alike, smiling and laughing. And why not? He wasn't a regular pedophile. He was a *forgiven* pedophile.

I myself didn't even feel forgiven. I was still filthy from wrongdoing I hadn't confessed to. I had enjoyed homosexual sex on occasion, and the elders didn't know, so I couldn't be forgiven. Funny how sexual abuse makes one feel. Can't scrub that shit off, ever.

From the outside, though, you couldn't tell I was filthy. Many Jehovah's Witnesses are poor materially, but many are anything but. I had been raised to give Jehovah my best, and that meant a shiny exterior. Some occasions for new clothes for sure were all assembly and convention events as well as the memorial. It was the night to commemorate the memorial of the death of Christ.

The Kingdom Hall was typically packed for the memorial. We needed to look our best for any interested ones. Interested ones could be just random ones in attendance but were to be treated as if they were interested enough to one day be our brother or sister in the fold.

Fashion became somewhat of a competition between sisters. In particular, one sister approached me often and wanted to know how much I had paid for my shoes, bag, or whatever. She was quick to point out if I had gotten something on sale if she had seen it on a sale rack. Stupid exchanges, really, if one considers what God's house is really for.

Gossip was forbidden in the Kingdom Hall, but there were always unhealthy doses of it. In the car group for ministry, it was definitely gossip central. Despite a "local needs" part instructing car captains to nip gossip in the bud, the problem persisted. Each month the governing organization who decides what the programs for spiritual instruction will include, leaves a slot open for local elders to determine what spiritual instruction is needed locally. One such local need talk from the stage had a live demonstration of how to handle the problem. Instructing us on how to shoot down negative talk, they acknowledged that it was a real problem. Interesting, though, was the fact that the elder giving the talk was quite the offender in that area.

Gays in particular were made fun of often. Gays—or, as my dad would say, "people a little light in their loafers." One day, while out in the ministry, one sister saw a rainbow flag bumper sticker with no wording on it. She was an older sister, so I wasn't surprised when she asked what that could possibly stand for. "It's the queers that show their pride in their filthy lifestyle that way" was the answer that came from the back of the car. My heart sank instantly as I recalled the last girl I had dated. She was a sweet girl, but not one I would ever leave my life and embarrass my family for. Still, I hurt for her; she was openly gay, and there I was, aligning myself with bigots. I don't feel justified in the fact that I was desperate to stay in what I thought was the only true religion and that I assumed would save my life and the life of my child.

McAlester is a small town. I had no desire to be outed there. People in the congregation looked up to my family. We were steadfastly spiritual and private. That was our reputation. Sunday meetings were usually followed by family lunches out. I actually anticipated those lunches, and it was disappointing when we couldn't all go. Our discussions were intelligent and thorough. I say thorough because it seemed to me at the time that we discussed things from all angles, and I enjoyed it.

Careful not to question the teachings of the Society, I did sometimes express opinions my family didn't fully agree with. One such Sunday, when I insisted on disagreeing, my dad became furious. "Shut your mouth, Debbie." I don't even recall what the disagreement was concering. I only recall it angered my father when I voiced the disagreement.

"I won't," I replied. I did feel a little beneath my sister and father at times. My father was brilliant, and my sister mirrored him perfectly. She lived for his approval and scarcely made a move without his input. She was the brains in her family. Her husband, a devoted workhorse, was more like myself: fewer brains but willing to work. Hard work never deterred me, and that is the case with most Jehovah's Witnesses. In their training, they are taught the idea that when God destroys the wicked at Armageddon, the earth will be a mess, complete with dead bodies of non-JWs piled high. We would have to be willing to clean up the global murder scene.

I began having trouble with the concept of it. I knew a lot of stellar people. Stellar people who kindly but firmly rejected teachings of Jehovah's Witnesses. Were they, too, slated for murder by God? Worse than that, Ronnie was forgiven with a free pass to paradise?

With Jehovah's Witnesses, though, if you disagree or doubt, you should act quickly to root out your rebellious spirit. Ideally, the organization would expect you to pray to root out your insubordinance and read literature dispensed by the organization until you have no doubts. You cannot let it fester, or you're in danger of apostasy, and apostasy is unforgivable. Do not read dissenting opinions. It's dangerous. I can remember as a child the apostates (those who denounce the faith) Jehovah's Witnesses after being baptized) protesting outside our convention hall. I was ushered away by my mother. We, as children, were instructed to not even glance at them. Yes, I agreed. I agreed at eight years of age that these were bad, demon-filled people deserving of death.

Something is terribly wrong when a child can be manipulated into judging another's heart and standing with God. I wouldn't say that whether you believe in God or not is completely irrelevant to me. It's relevant. I hope you do. However, it is wholly your business. If you hate Jehovah's Witness beliefs, I happen to agree. It's still none of my business. Who you love, sleep with, marry, worship—you get the idea—is none of my business.

Jehovah's Witness parents gleam with pride if they have successfully manipulated the minds of their children. "Like arrows in the quiver of a mighty man," is a verse from Psalm 127 and they claim mind "adjustments" of their children simply facilitate the straight shot of their little arrows.

As an adult, I lived in fear. The fear was not daily, but it certainly recurred persistently. Did it matter that I wasn't fully out of the closet? Surely God knew my filthiness even if the elders did not. So there I was, living in a disapproved condition. With Jehovah's

Witnesses, if you are living one way but your heart is inclined another way, you may as well be disfellowshiped. So, everywhere I looked, I still felt inferior. The obese sister who couldn't stop eating—better than me. The exuberant pioneer sister who threw buckets of ice water on her kids so they could rise at 5:00 a.m. to read scripture—better than me. (Yes, she was real. Scary, but real.) Worst of all, Ronnie, the forgiven pedophile—better than me.

I desperately clung to my pioneer status. It boosted my self-esteem. I had decided to devote seventy hours a month to the field ministry and there was a status of sorts that came with that.

Like it or not, there is a hierarchy within the organization. All officers must be men. The members of the governing body in New York City are top dogs and are going to heaven. They are followed by Bethelites, who dedicate their lives to serve at the organization's world headquarters in New York City. These people usually forego the idea of children and, many times, marriage. It was on good authority that those serving at Bethel were told to use three forms of birth control to be sure they didn't get pregnant and sent home. Such people struggle to make ends meet, finding it hard to find employment with no education and no savings. College educations are frowned on within the organization and therefore, parents discourage their children from pursuing those educations, feeling the end of the world will come before they can benefit from higher education. The more you sacrifice, the higher you are esteemed. Just under Bethel servants are district overseers, who oversee more than one circuit of congregations.

Then, you have circuit overseers. These are traveling brothers who come to "assist elders in guiding the flock." I will say it's quite comical to see someone suck up to a circuit overseer. Twice a year, a circuit overseer and usually his spouse visit the congregations they are assigned to. They do that for about three years before being reassigned. They aren't to establish relationships. One overseer made no bones about it. "I'm not here to make friends," he said. No, he wasn't. He was visiting to ensure the congregation was putting in adequate service hours and to make sure no wrongdoing was being left unpunished. Perhaps the congregation needed a good purging. If left undone, the Holy Spirit would cease to flow to that congregation and perhaps the circuit. I suppose all those years that Ronnie was at the peak of his game put quite a crimp in the flow of Holy Spirit.

Circuit overseers are superior to local bodies of elders. Elders wield relative power. They have the power to remove wrongdoers but don't really do so without consulting the Society. They are puppets of the branch office, really. Yet, elders still have enough power to instill fear in the members of the flock. They are to be obeyed as if they themselves are the governing body.

Elders' become elders on approval from the branch office after praying over the recommendation.

One step down is ministerial servants. Servants are usually younger men who seek to someday be elders. One exception I noted was an older man who started over as a servant when ousted from his elder status. He had cheated on his wife numerous times and then qualified to be only a servant now. Like elders, servants' wives have to be kept in check for the brother to qualify for the privilege. One ministerial servant friend of mine lost his privilege because his wife was awful. She truly was. She took no lip at all from her servant husband, and they fought often. Their arguments became a topic of conversation among the friends in the congregation. One day, in my car in the ministry, she slapped him. I drove them back to their cars, disgusted with them both. *Just get out. Give me a break from you. We will resume this torture tomorrow.*

Next class distinction: regular pioneers. At one time, pioneers were devoted to getting ninety hours of ministry in a month; the requirement was reduced to seventy hours. Just putting in 70 hours though will not do. To become a regular pioneer you must apply and be reviewed for stellar behavior before being appointed to such a position. God love my mother and her pioneering. She hurt a lot. She didn't sleep well and yet showed up as a pioneer with more dedication than most. She didn't enjoy the work, though. She felt a bit as I did: like a door-to-door salesman. Often, we would have campaigns in the ministry. Campaigns were a quick-moving blanketing of our assigned territory. On these occasions, we were encouraged to walk more quickly from house to house and leave a tract or an invitation for the householder. In campaigns, it wasn't necessary to actually speak with the homeowner. It was to be a quick moving campaign. This activity weighed on Mom. As a general rule, flip-flops were frowned on as something only a spiritually weak person would wear in the ministry, but many resorted to that footwear as a more comfortable option for campaigns. Not my mom, though. She was the picture of dignity in her ministry.

I won't say that at times pioneers didn't feel superior to others. We absolutely did. We put in hard hours in the field. Those who didn't pioneer were considered slackers and weak. Twice yearly, we benefited from an exclusive invitation to the Pioneer Session (a meeting comprised of a series of talks meant to train ones in the field ministry). Nonpioneers were not welcome to attend.

All in all, pioneers had an inflated view of self. I wondered why it was we couldn't celebrate our birthdays, though, since it would give us an inflated view of self. Birthdays were considered to be a day when the birthday boy or girl thought only about themselves and that was unacceptable. I never asked anyone the question. I feared being labeled a possible apostate in the making.

There were many good times in our little group of pioneers. We, in general, were looked up to. While it's true we worked hard, we could also let loose and be inappropriate. My sarcastic sense of humor leaned toward jokes of a sexual nature. One pioneer in particular was, for lack of a better word, a bitch. Single and unhappy about it, she was jealous of anyone who had something she didn't. She was miserable and made others miserable. I avoided her whenever possible. She found me ridiculous and was pretty obvious about it. She came by it naturally. Her parents were stoically unhappy people. Regular pioneers are supposed to be happier than she was. At least, we kept getting told to be happier than others. Our gleam of happiness would encourage others to pioneer.

The next group is auxiliary pioneers. They put in fifty hours a month in the field but still are not welcome at regular pioneer meetings. Next, you have your average publisher. A publisher is approved to go in the ministry and has been baptized, having proven to the elders he is free of bad habits such as tobacco use. Knock back as much alcohol as you wish, short of drunkenness, but no tobacco, please. Next is the publisher not yet baptized. These are typically new members. They are not approved for baptism yet but have proven to be free of vices and are approved for the ministry if they are people of good reputation. Baptism wasn't as simple as in some other religions. It was a tedious process of quaifications to meet. If affiliated with any other religion, they must submit a letter of resignation to their previous church, even if they were a child when joining it. Sometimes, I wanted to start over at that rank and then just fade away into oblivion. I could find a nice little wife for myself and be left alone. If I never got baptized, I couldn't be disfellowshipped and being disfellowshipped is simply one of the most disgusting, humiliating, torturous things I can thing of for one to endure.

My husband had progressed in the organization despite having been a Baptist previously. He was an elder. It was imperative that I maintain the impression that our little family was exemplary in all aspects of life. Word came down from the organization to the congregations that it would now be required of family heads to hold a weekly worship with their families at home. If they wanted their loved ones to survive Armageddon, they would be diligent about doing so. Chuck couldn't have cared less, yet I took the mandate very seriously. I waited for him to comply. It didn't happen. I took over the planning of it. He would sit in but would stare blankly, rarely saying a word. I grew frustrated but knew saying anything would reveal my lack of submission; it was also embarrassing that he hadn't complied quickly. After all, it supposedly meant our lives. The word from the organization was not unclear. "Family worship will mean the difference between your survival or your destruction at the coming Armageddon." Maybe my life wasn't valuable to him. *But our daughter's should be*, I thought. Sisters weren't to handle matters of this nature, so I phoned my dad to complain. He was disgusted but could do little.

Marley got baptized at age eleven despite my apprehension. By all accounts, we were the perfect family. My immediate family knew, of course, that Chuck and I separated often. Chuck always refused to leave the home, stating that if I didn't want to be in the marriage, I would have to be the one to leave and that I should be prepared to leave with nothing. So, I often stayed at hotels or at the homes of friends. They knew that even when I returned home to him, I had created a little room for myself in my closet. I had a little chair that pulled out into a bed, and I slept there often. It got to the point that even hearing my husband pull up after work made me agitated. We didn't fight in the typical sense, but there was always tension in the air. I admitted infidelity, and although we decided to try to stay together, it was not at all what I wanted.

He liked having the wife I tried to be—the wife who cooked, cleaned, and so on. I didn't mind those parts of it, either. I just didn't fit, though. I tried, and I tried hard. The desire to perform traditional wifely duties escaped me. Sexually, it just seemed an obligation. It was always just short of what I could grasp.

My hair, my dress, and my choices reflected that I was always a little left of center. I was not quite right, especially in JW land. I persisted in trying not to form worldly friendships, not to don immodest attire, and not to sport a too-manly haircut. I was counseled on that last one more than once.

My hairdresser was a sister from a congregation an hour and a half away. She was good at what she did, but after about three years of making the trip, I grew tired of it and looked for recommendations closer to home. Someone suggested a girl I had actually gone to high school with. Tina booked my appointment over the phone, happily saying she would see me soon.

On the day of my appointment, I went to the salon a little nervously. I didn't like being in crowds of worldly people, and the salon was busy. As soon as I walked in, I saw a girl I had first seen at a restaurant years ago. She had obviously been on a date with who appeared to be her girlfriend.

I remembered thinking to myself, *That is the prettiest woman I have ever seen in my life.* She noticed me staring and looked at me like I was rude. After that, I had seen her occasionally at the local coffeehouse but wouldn't look at her long. There was no point. Yes, she was pretty, but I was a JW—and a married one, at that. I busied myself with Kingdom interests. That would do the trick, or so my mom always said. Despite being devoted to the

Witnesses, though, I was not devoted to my husband, and he knew it. It isn't that I hated him as much as I just felt like a square peg in a round hole. My solution was to live a life that didn't really include him. If he got too close to me sexually or emotionally, I would pack Marley up and leave for my parents' house. Many times, I would begin to feel bad about my behavior and return home. Divorce was constantly in my thoughts.

My new hairstylist worked across from the pretty girl from the restaurant. Crystal was her name. After about four or five bad experiences with my hairdresser, I joined my boss's daughter for a trip to the salon. Crystal cut her hair. On the way there, I had expressed my frustration with my stylist. Still, I was surprised that she asked Crystal to take me on as a client. She seemed unfazed by the request and casually made me an appointment. I was nervous and didn't fully understand why.

Crystal was dating someone. I was staying in touch with another girl a few hours away. However, I thought that it would be nice to have Crystal as a friend. We became fast friends. We chatted easily at my appointments. Crystal went through a breakup and then entered a new relationship. She seemed happy, and I was happy for her.

We began communicating between salon appointments. Texting, mostly. Even when I was in the door-to-door work, we kept in touch. My mother and pioneer associates hated the friendship and warned me about how lesbians take straight people and turn them gay. That was Satan's way. I laughed inside while pretending to take them seriously. *I doubt she will be changing me. If JWs can't do it, Crystal isn't going to do it.*

I was afraid of developing feelings beyond friendship, but she didn't seem interested in a relationship. Still, I was attracted to her. I cancelled my next hair appointment. She didn't ask why, and I wasn't surprised she didn't. She always had her mind on other things. She had her own problems. She didn't know about me, and I liked it that way. Months passed, and we had sporadic conversations via text. I made an appointment. Something in me missed her. I didn't really want to hear about the love of her life, but I listened and encouraged her.

She discussed moving closer to where her girlfriend lived.

I said, "I won't travel to use you."

She said, "Yes, you will."

I would have. Luckily she never made that move.

Our texts became more and more frequent until there were dozens a day. I felt them harmless, although

JWs would say they were anything but. Homosexuality aside, even the worldly association was deadly. I didn't care. She was my friend. Unfortunately, she was the first thing I thought of in the morning and the last thing I thought of at night.

Occasionally, she would visit my home on Sunday afternoons. Crystal's Sunday visits were considered wrong. A worldly person isn't to socialize at the home of a Witness. Later, Chuck would be removed as elder, partly because he "allowed" the visits. She would talk to me while I cooked, just being a friend to me. Her girlfriend somehow had stopped being her girlfriend. Crystal wasn't sure why, and wasn't happy about it.

Our conversations only increased. She had stopped drinking and changed many of her habits such as drinking and partying hoping to better herself and her outlook on life. She wanted something different for her life, but she was currently heartbroken. I checked on her often, and she seemed to appreciate it.

Hand to God, she did not cause the demise of my marriage. It was dead in the water from the start. What Chuck needed was a good ol' redneck girl and in our area of the world that usually is synonymous with a submissive, traditional wife, not me. We got into an argument so bad that I packed a bag and drove an hour and a half to Tulsa to stay the night. I was tired of bothering my parents for a place to sleep. Besides, Marley was away with them for the weekend. Doubletree was my choice. It was not my first visit.

Crystal texted when I was almost to Tulsa. She didn't ask why I had gone. She simply said, "I'll be there as soon as I get off work." She would make the drive to Tulsa from McAlester which was 90 miles away. We both lived in McAlester but frequented Tulsa, as there was just more to do in Tulsa.

"OK." I never thought twice about it. *She's my friend. I care for her. I'll tell not a soul.*

She picked me up at my hotel. As was typical, we chatted easily. We went to dinner. She was still coping with her breakup.

"Relationships suck," I said. Mine was no exception. I confided in her that I had not been faithful.

Then, there it was—out of the blue, the question. "Did you cheat with men or with women when you cheated?" she asked.

"Women."

A pin drop would have been a welcome sound.

We changed the subject. As the evening went on, there was not much mention of it, yet I felt like an idiot for my admission. I didn't want to lose my friendship to any awkwardness. By the end of the evening, I knew I hadn't. The night ended well, and she dropped me off at my hotel. Glancing at my overnight bag, I knew then that if I returned to him, it would only be for Marley's sake.

My relationship with Crystal, whatever it would be, was what I needed. However, our friendship was somehow different. For the first time, I had opened up to another person. We talked about everything, with one exception: Ronnie. She, too, had been abused but not to the extent I had, and I wasn't ready to disclose it.

We both felt strongly that we had not been born gay. When in the company of those who had been, I felt a little embarrassed to say that I hadn't. Natural-born gays take pride in that fact that they are natural born gays. It becomes a sticking point between homosexuals and those who feel homosexuality is a choice. Although I feel I wasn't born that way, I definitely feel I didn't choose it. I feel it chose me. In the male-dominant organization, women are to be submissive, and while they by and large are treated with respect, they still must know their place, always. After my experience with men, I was not interested in male dominance.

The elders, for instance, have a manual for shepherding the flock. Sisters are under strict instruction to not even peek inside this book. Now, why would a simple manual for shepherding be confidential? Sisters were not to carry out duties designated for brothers. Yet, at one time, my mother took care of the congregation bookkeeping, despite the fact that we had our fair share of servants and elders in the congregation. My dad said there was not a single brother capable of the task, and with that, he gave the assignment to Mother.

Dad often seemed frustrated that other brothers were somehow lacking in their qualifications, even ones supposedly appointed to positions by the Holy Spirit. I wondered if the Holy Spirit had in such appointments. On another occasion, my dad needed help handing out newly released publications at a district convention. He asked me, along with other pioneer sisters, to hand out books. This was typically done only by qualified brothers. The crowd formed lines, eagerly awaiting their copies. As I handed a book to one brother in line, he said, "What has this organization come to, letting women hand out books?" Bigotry and chauvinistic behavior was absolutely rampant.

I enjoyed my role as pioneer, though. I was good at it. Once at a pioneer meeting, which the elders held annually, an elder commended me on my ability to persuade others toward God's true religion. I was proud.

Now, I feel I need to return to all the people's homes where I tried to "persuade" them. I owe them an apology.

Once, when I was meeting with a Bible student, she confided in me that her husband was beating her. She asked if she could scripturally divorce him. I said, "You can, but if you remarry and he hasn't slept with someone else, you will be guilty of adultery." She was shocked and upset. I didn't blame her. I was repeating what I'd been taught, not what I knew to be God's feelings on the subject.

Furthermore, I was a hypocrite.

I've thought of her often since then. I hope she has left and found happiness.

My mother and I regularly traveled to Tulsa. We enjoyed days away from pioneering. We got to dress casually and do some shopping, always stopping to enjoy a nice meal before returning to the grind of our lives. If we were behind on our time reports (pioneers needed 840 hours a year), we would drop *The Watchtower* and *Awake!* magazines off with someone as we left town, starting our time. Reportable field service time couldn't begin to accumulate until something spiritual had been done. The Watchtower society expects their congregants to keep very good track of time spent ministering and turn it in monthly. We would make frequent stops along the way, offering the magazines to keep our time going. I hated it, and Mother hated it. The time had to be kept up, though. If we had a doctor's appointment, we would strike up a conversation with anyone sitting close to us and try to place literature as we had been trained for so long to do. In our training, they likened not witnessing to people we encountered to sailing past a drowning person and not rendering aid. You had to throw a lifeline.

Talk about pressure.

If any non-Witness was drowning, and we didn't witness, we were guilty. If we threw a lifeline and it was rejected, then that was another matter entirely—the loss of their life at Armageddon wasn't our problem.

My sister and I often discussed various lines of reasoning by the Society. For every spiritual topic, the organization offers "lines of reasoning", or ways of explaining in a convincing way why you believe the way you do. Being raised in the Society was through no choice of our own, so were we just lucky or specifically chosen by God?

It was on one of our trips to Tulsa that my mother began to question me about my friendship with Crystal. "You know it's inappropriate," she said.

"I know, Mom."

I very much believed I was in the wrong and that I would likely soon die at Armageddon anyway. No matter all my hard work in service, all my study, and all my meeting attendance, I was still filthy.

I voiced that to Mother. "I'm just bad, Mom. I'm sorry."

Her reply: "Try harder."

Silently, I protested. *Mom, I'm gay, and you know it. I love her.* She already knew I loved her, though.

A couple of months later, Crystal and I expressed love for one another. We had not yet been intimate.

I decided to be honest with everyone who seemed to care. Oh, what the hell—I'd be honest with Dad too. Little did I know what lay ahead of me for that choice. Approaching my dad was more nerve-wracking than approaching my husband, but somehow I felt I owed him that. He seemed to only care about his reputation and the reputation of his family. He let me know I would regret my decision, and, boy, did he mean it. I told my husband I was finally leaving and wouldn't be back this time. Not only that, but I was also leaving the organization. Anyone even remotely affiliated with that organization knows what all that entails.

Understandably, my husband was upset. Who wants to lose a good workhorse? Ignorantly, I had assumed that as an adult, I could make this choice free of reprisal. I was dead wrong.

Chuck assumed I would be back and texted me many times to that effect, so we agreed to share custody of Marley. No paperwork was immediately filed to reflect that agreement, which was a mistake on my part.

I found an apartment not far from work. Crystal and I looked forward to time together and to telling Marley. The feeling of a free life was great. The promise of freedom was sweet but wasn't to come for some time. In spite of my freedom, I still felt very much Jehovah's Witness to the core. It was the only true religion on planet earth. I just didn't, *couldn't* fit in there.

To say Jehovah's Witnesses were rocked by my exit would be a vast understatement. Elders began to call continuously, even ones from other congregations, asking to pray with me. One night, I lay on the floor of my mostly empty apartment and fell asleep while on the phone with an elder. His prayer went largely unheard, not because I lacked appreciation for his efforts but because I couldn't hold my eyes open. Sleep was a luxury I wasn't afforded any longer. My hair began to fall out. Stress was my constant companion. My nerves were shot to hell.

Jehovah's Witnesses would say (and did) that I brought all this on myself. Circuit overseers, their wives, and their friends from all over began to call. Those who didn't call sure did talk about it, though. Rumors in a small town are like wildfire, and it doesn't matter if they are true. The stories got more absurd every day. I had lost my mind. I actually had several children, and I had abandoned them to be with a woman who was bad news. *Maybe it was that anesthesia from a recent procedure she had. She hasn't been right since then. She doesn't know reality from fiction.* The rumors were endless.

Chuck and Crystal exchanged hateful texts. Chuck and I exchanged hateful texts. My only comfort came when I could get to my apartment. It had a garage attached to it. I could pull in and go in the house without ever seeing daylight. A friend and his wife lived right next door. I took comfort in that. We were not close friends to the extent we socialized, yet I felt safe knowing I could call on them if ever a need arose.

Crystal and I were excited about the possibility of a future vastly different from the one we had thought we were locked into. We both had spent years pursuing a way of life that wasn't the best for us and we were ready for a change. She began to spend the night often, but we were scared, and rightly so.

Chuck, my sister, and my family started a campaign, the goal of which was clear: relieve me of my parental rights and turn Marley against her mother.

At the beginning of my separation from Chuck, Marley was with me virtually every day as he worked. My job was far more flexible, and she could go with me. He would get her half the time that he was off work.

Marley was twelve. From the moment she was born to me, I took being her parent very seriously, and I was a damn good mother—stellar, actually, rivaling even my mother's parenting from when I was a child. Chuck had been involved in her parenting very little. That is somewhat typical in rural Oklahoma. Men work long hours. Women try to work less in order to care for the kids and the house. To hear my dad's opinion of the ordeal would be a little different. *Women shouldn't work at all, if possible. School the kids at home. Take care of wifely things. Keeping up appearances is a full-time job.* It was his encouragement and seeing my sister's success at home-schooling that prompted me to homeschool Marley.

The pending divorce proved very difficult for Marley. Her schoolwork seemed to suffer, as she was unable to focus. It wasn't for lack of trying. She asked if she could sit in on my sister's homeschool classes, and I acquiesced.

Soon, my family decided I was no longer fit to school Marley or, in fact, parent her. On one outing to my former residence, I found some papers Chuck had filled out with the help of a local elder. He had filed them with the Watchtower Society. *Debbie is no longer morally or mentally fit to parent her child.*

Marley was angry with me for the whole mess. I would've been angry too. But what followed was the stuff movies are made of. She was suddenly a very difficult, embittered child. She would yell at me. "I hate you and want to be with my dad and never see you again!" These words broke me in two.

Acting out was an understatement. She began to speak of suicide if I didn't return home. I tried to explain to her that this was not an easy decision and that time would heal these wounds.

I couldn't go back. Doing so would kill me. I was sure of it. Chuck, who had previously spoken very little to either Marley or me, all of a sudden seemed the involved parent. His texts would vary from very sweet and kind—*Come back; I miss you*—to *You know you're going to pay for this decision.* I was scared all the time.

Crystal never stayed at the apartment overnight when Marley was there. We knew this would be a tough transition and didn't want to make it harder than it was already.

I was at the house packing some things for the move when Chuck called. "You really gonna do this?"

"I am."

"Have you told Marley yet that you're a queer?"

"Not yet."

"When I get home, I'm just gonna have a nice chat with her, then."

No! That is not *yours to tell. That belongs to me.* It is common in that organization, though, for people to tell things that aren't theirs to tell.

I panicked and asked Marley to come talk with me. My voice shook as I told her what I was. I was shocked by her reaction. "OK, Mom. It's OK."

Her acceptance infuriated Chuck. The world hadn't stopped spinning, and Marley still loved her mother.

I believe this acceptance is what led them all to amp up their campaign efforts against me. Things got worse from that moment. Even when Chuck had Marley, he used his time to follow Crystal and me and sit outside my apartment.

An elder requested a meeting. Had I been a wiser person and less of a coward, I would've said, "Sir, this is none of your business, and no, there will be no meeting about my private business." Instead I heard myself say, "Yes, sir, I'll be there."

In many respects, I am like my mother: generally mild tempered and not prone to fits of anger. Back then, I was worried about being impolite or hurting someone's feelings, even if that person disliked me or had proven to be an asshole. I wanted to be liked.

Saying yes to the meeting was in fact still my show of submission to what JWs call theocratic order. Theocratic order dictated that I be cross-examined by a judicial committee regarding my actions. So I went. Chuck was present. Intimate questions from the committee made me shiver with nervousness. Bibles out; notebooks and pens ready. *Yes, brothers, let's add to my already thick file. You know, the large one next to Tommy's where all the worthless ones are kept.*

Despite my nerves, when they mentioned Crystal's name, I smiled. Thinking silently about her, I wasn't absorbing how bad this deal was about to get.

A judicial committee is appointed to get the facts and decide if one is repentant. At the end of the day, the committee will decide if you are worthy to remain in the congregation or need to be disfellowshiped.

Raised JW, I had been dedicated and baptized at the age of thirteen and that is considered the entering of a legal contract with God and the organization. I had begun preparations to do so about age eight. In Oklahoma, you can drive at sixteen. At eighteen, you can enter some legal contracts. At twenty-one, you can purchase alcohol. Even then, most would agree that people are not mentally equipped to devote the rest of their lives to something or someone. But there I sat, on the verge of being disfellowshiped again because of a thirteen-year-old decision to be baptized. If I had never been baptized, there could be no disfellowshiping—no dedication and baptism, no shunning. But that was spilled milk.

They reminded me of my dedication to God and his earthly representative, the organization. If I had dedicated myself to God, why not leave God and me to work out my sins and my homosexuality?

They asked probing questions about how far Crystal and I had gone sexually and if I had had an orgasm. One elder interrupted me before I could answer. "Be careful with your answer. Your answer could mean spiritual suicide here."

Fuck you, I thought. *My spirituality is my business.*

I didn't answer them. I did, though, tell them I was offended that they would expect me to reveal personal information, not just about me but about her as well. I told them if they wanted to know about our sex life, they could invite her in and ask her. They looked at each other as if to say, *She has lost it.* After all, a worldly person would never be invited to a theocratic meeting of such weight. He or she wouldn't understand.

They were right in a way. I was losing it. Losing respect for a religion. Losing respect for an organization I had worked my ass off for, which in return had repeatedly protected a pedophile.

They asked me what Crystal was like, and I told them she was actually quite a spiritual person, even church-going. One elder laughed at me. "Does she know, then, what God's laws are on this disgusting lifestyle?"

That is your interpretation of scripture, sir.

I left the meeting in a fog. I was exhausted. Crystal and I had plans for that evening to have dinner, but right then, she was working. I had some Ambien my mother had given me. I reasoned I could take a couple (one seldom worked) and sleep for several hours. I needed it. My mind reeled from the first judicial proceeding. As I took the pills, I remember Chuck texting me. He was worried about me. I didn't seem OK to him as I had left the Kingdom Hall. Hell no, I wasn't OK. *Leave me alone.*

The next thing I remember, I awoke in the hospital with the chalky taste of charcoal in my mouth and bits of it in my teeth. It was a blur of activity. The elders were waiting outside along with my family. Chuck and my dad were standing by my bed. *What the...*

I needed a moment to try to figure out what has happened. It turned out that when I didn't reply to Chuck's texts, he had called the police and an ambulance. With two Ambien in my system, I was out. Really out. I had no recollection of the ambulance ride.

"I just wanted a nap! Someone hear me on this!"

Crystal appeared in the doorway. Chuck says now that he knew by the look on my face when I saw her there that this was a done deal.

They admitted me to ICU, which is standard procedure for attempted suicides. *Attempted suicide? No!* I was to be transferred to a psychiatric facility the next morning. I asked the nurse if I could walk out. She smiled. "You can try, but there's security for that." My heart sank. The nurse seemed to recognize the situation. She asked if I wanted to allow or not allow anyone in as visitors. *Absolutely. Please do not allow anyone but Crystal in here to see me.* At least I had some rights.

Two other friends who were non-JWs were also welcome. *No Jehovah's Witnesses in here.* I thought of a friend who could likely help. I phoned him. He was also a baptized Witness but had left when he began to question the teachings. He said he would try to help.

Within forty-five minutes of my phone call to my friend, I was being discharged. Like never before, I knew this was really going to be an ugly, scary ordeal. The gravity of my situation settled in on me at various times throughout the ordeal with Jehovah's Witnesses and this was sure one of them.

The elders phoned. I was to be disfellowshiped. They had driven by my apartment, and upon seeing Crystal's car there, they knew I wasn't willing to break off ties with her as they had instructed.

I was determined not to return to the organization this time. The longer I held out, the worse things became. I began to get letters in the mail from members of the congregation damning me to a terrible death at Armageddon. Hate letters became a regular occurrence, some even being sent certified mail.

My family began to tell Marley, who was by then fourteen, that I was like a hog in a pen and that she couldn't be around me and remain morally clean. She agreed, and it came to the point that she would not return my texts or visit my home. A custody agreement wasn't in place at this point, so I couldn't force her. I tried every day. When I moved some of my furniture out of the house Chuck and I had shared, Marley did call. “Put the furniture back, and I will speak to you again.”

I let myself be manipulated time after time by her. I was desperate to have her affections back. She said that if I wanted to see her, I had to go to the house Chuck and I had shared and spend the night. On a couple of occasions, I did. It was very, very creepy, though. Once, I was asleep in Marley’s bed with her and awoke to see Chuck standing over me. It was the last time I went.

As the days passed, I found life impossible to cope with without my child. Crystal did the best she could, but I was a basket case. I lost a lot of weight. It was similar to my anorexia days when weak was all I knew. Crystal took me to dinner. While there, I ran into a friend of mine. Mark was an attorney in town and, from all I knew, a good one. We discussed the schemes of my parents and soon-to-be ex-husband. He took me on as a client. The first order of business was to order depositions to be taken with Dad and Chuck. His goal was to expose exactly what they were trying to do and get my daughter back to me.

It was going to be a rocky road.

Marley visited some during these weeks of legal wrangling. She became obsessed with the fact she didn’t know how lesbian sex worked. I told her that given her age, I didn't feel it appropriate to go into the specifics of it. Not knowing seemed to infuriate her.

Early one morning, I awoke to Marley standing next to my bed. "Tell me, Mom. I have to know."

I was frustrated. Marley had always before taken no for an answer with little fuss. "What do you want us to do? Do it in front of you? Stop asking!" It probably wasn't the best reply, but nerves had gotten the better of me.

Marley left the following day to spend the weekend with her dad. I phoned him to see when she would be back. "She won't be back, and you will never see her again" was his reply.

"What? What are you talking about?" I pleaded. Click. I called Marley's phone. Click. Then, there was no answer at either number. Over and over, I phoned. Occasionally, they would pick up and immediately hang up. My attorney texted on Monday. *Chuck is not bringing Marley because apparently you are a pedophile now. You offered to have sex with Crystal in front of Marley?*

I swear, the room began to spin. Spiraling mentally, I was desperate to speak with Chuck. He knew better! Why was my child saying these things? Finally, she answered her phone. She was angry. "Mom, you shouldn't have said that. Now they have you."

Wow. Now I saw what I was up against. They would stop at nothing. I wrote Dad a letter. In it, I expressed my disgust with him. I told him even if I was ever reinstated, I would never utter another word to him. The elders called the Department of Human Services and reported my "crime." After days of ignoring my phone calls, Chuck finally answered his phone and informed me of the elders action. Funny that Ronnie was never reported. The idea that I was being accused of possible sexual misconduct rattled not only my brain but my entire body. It was unspeakable. I sat stunned, paralyzed and disgusted.

My attorney did his job. The depositions he took with my dad and Chuck revealed exactly who they were. Even their attorneys were embarrassed. Dad was not one to hide that he was a man of God. He, on many occasions, claimed ecclesiastical privilege. It didn't work.

A court date was set. Crystal was instructed not to be present. Chuck, however, had his support system with him. My family, dressed fantastically, was all there with their little file folders, ready to testify that I was a unfit parent. It was a habit of many Witnesses and certainly my family, to document events as they interpreted them and drawing conclusions they felt would benefit them in any court case. The judge never heard from them in my divorce case. They had no legal rights to even be involved. It wasn't something my dad was used to. His presence would not be required. I'm quite sure he was appalled.

The judge didn't want to hear my horror stories of the past six months. He asked Chuck's lawyer to present any kind of evidence proving I could not parent. They had none. The judge seemed irritated. He said, "Give me evidence of something, and I'll investigate it. If you've got nothing, then you will cooperate with a joint custody arrangement." And so it was. Joint custody on paper, finally.

Marley wanted nothing to do with it, though, and made that known. The first few days back with me, she made it very difficult. She was very disrespectful and would simply walk away when I told her what to do. One day, she was especially unkind. I went to my bedroom, shut the door, and cried in bed. Crystal came home and, seeing the obvious problem, decided to have a talk with Marley. Marley tried to walk out of the room, and Crystal put her hand in the air. "You're not walking out while I'm talking," she said. Marley walked into her hand. Lightly.

Crystal left. A few minutes later, the doorbell rang, and Marley came to tell me I had company. The police were at the door. *Oh dear God, help me.* My eyes were swollen from crying. The policeman stated that he had been called to my home because Crystal had physically assaulted Marley.

Marley's anger was making her do very mean things that were in no way, shape, or form correct or warranted. She was mad because I grounded her from her phone. She used an app on her iPad to contact my sister, who in turn phoned the police. I couldn't contact my sister with my shunned status. I wanted to. I did text her. *Stay out of my life!*

That night was one that I did not sleep. I had had enough. I rose early, and when I walked into the police station, I was clear. "I'm not leaving here until someone helps me with the harassment from Jehovah's Witnesses."

One thing I want to convey is this: Marley is and always has been an amazing person. I never in any way blamed her for her behavior. When a person or an organization plays with the mind of a child, it isn't the fault of the child.

The police were willing to hear me out. What followed was hours of pouring out information: all the hate letters being sent, all the harassment, all the lies, all the JW bullshit that I was no longer able to take. I pleaded for their help. In my conversation with police, I said, "You know, you would think that an organization that protected a pedophile would just let one of his victims go quietly."

That got their attention, even though I didn't expect it to. It's not why I was there. It had honestly never occurred to me to go to the police with that part of my story. Ironically, if the organization hadn't spent the last six months torturing me, I never would've even walked into that police station.

They asked for a formal statement, and I gave it. It wasn't very cleansing to tell it. I knew that with Jehovah's Witnesses, if you tell something confidential, especially of any significance, you are then deemed an apostate. The unforgivable sin. It scared me to think I was in that position now.

A detective called with a request for a meeting. I told him all I remembered about the molestation. To my pleasant surprise, he took my testimony quite seriously as he set about contacting the other victims.

It came to a point that the police needed proof that the local body of elders and the Watchtower Society knew of the abuse and did nothing but handle it internally. There had been no report to the authorities locally. Detectives had checked.

How could we prove they knew? The file. Dad was a meticulous record keeper, and I knew of the file. Every word ever uttered on this case was in the notes, locked in a file cabinet. The detectives requested and obtained a search warrant for the Kingdom Hall. They met with me to determine what the best time was to serve it. I knew Dad always attended field ministry on Tuesday mornings. He was there when they arrived to serve the warrant.

Brent, the lead detective on the case, phoned me from the Kingdom Hall foyer. "Where is the file cabinet?"

"In the elders' room, through the glass doors and to your immediate left."

"This file cabinet is empty, Debbie."

"No way."

A couple of days after leaving the Kingdom Hall empty-handed, Brent called again. Someone from the Kingdom Hall had phoned him and invited him back. He went. There was but one single file. The Ronnie file. He retrieved it.

In it, there was a wealth of substantiation of my claims. There was proof of all correspondence with the Society regarding Ronnie. Proof that they all knew of the sexual abuse. Proof the Society knew of it. Finally, there was a small feeling of vindication that I had not been crazy.

Ronnie was phoned by the detectives who requested a meeting with him. He came. I wasn't present for that meeting, but I was told he basically admitted the allegations were true. He was arrested and booked into the Pittsburg County jail. TV reporters came to McAlester, something they seldom needed to do. It was on television and in the newspaper. *Local man accused. Local church accused of a cover-up.*

Given my shunned status, I knew when I texted some of the elders involved following the local news that evening that I would not get a response. I simply said, *Maybe you should have thought of this before you chose to cover up a crime for forty years.* It was a mass text to my family and the elders. As I suspected, no reply came.

It was a cold night. Crystal and I were so pleased that Ronnie sat in jail. We went to bed. Sleep would only be fleeting, though. My thoughts? *He's an old man, and that jail is probably so cold. This is my fault. His poor, pitiful wife is home alone.* I soon discovered that many victims feel guilty when their abusers are held accountable.

His time in jail was also short-lived. Through the grapevine, we heard that Ronnie had been bailed out by a brother in the congregation. At the advice of my attorney, I closed my Facebook account. A friend, though, started sending me screenshots of the comments. Most Jehovah's Witnesses blasted me and the other victims.

This was shocking to me, despite my being the one ousted from the flock. The consensus of the comments was to leave the old man alone. The crimes were probably misunderstood by his victims and were just affection. How people are this ignorant floors me.

How many parents would blindly stand by and let their congregations handle these types of crimes? None should.

Within hours, I heard Ronnie had hired what was considered to be in our town a shark of a lawyer. I wasn't concerned. I had been assured by the assistant district attorney our case would be thoroughly proven; he wouldn't have been arrested if it hadn't been.

The problem with child abuse prosecutions many times is the statute of limitations. In our case, we were beyond that statute. However, there seemed to be a caveat to the statute that led the prosecutor and investigators to believe that the statute began "when authorities had been informed of the crimes." We had not been given the luxury of informing authorities immediately all those years ago. As a matter of fact, we had been coerced into not speaking of it, and the prosecutor wanted a chance to prove that to a judge. She would soon get her day.

As the hearing drew closer, I reached out to other victims. We needed each other now more than ever. I hesitated at first, thinking they were likely still part of the organization, but that wasn't the case. One detective on the case heard from one of them and relayed to me a request to reach out to her. It was Cissy. The original victim. The one who had the courage to come forward long before I did. We arranged to meet.

We didn't compare stories as much as we just relied on each other as a shoulder in what was now the toughest of times.

Months passed, and we were just determined to leave the issue in the court's hands. Wheels of justice grind slowly, we found.

In the summer of 2013, Crystal and I planned a vacation with some friends. Sailing seemed just what we needed to free ourselves from all we had been going through.

As always, I asked Marley to go with us. She wouldn't hear of it. My dad often was in charge of the drama (a play depicting a Bible story). These dramas are performed at the yearly district conventions of Jehovah's Witnesses. He had assigned her a role for the week we would be gone, and she was excited. The trip proved to be an excruciating time. I was tired of time away from Marley. She and I needed more time together, not less.

Marley was being told that time spent with me would only hinder my return to the organization. Still, I would beg for all the time I could get with her. The age of fourteen is a tough one, though, and she was still very angry. One day, I kept calling my mother's phone because I knew Marley was with her. She declined to answer many times in a row. However, she finally answered. "Mother, where is my daughter?" I asked angrily.

"I no longer answer to you. I answer to the brothers." The gravity of what I was up against hit me once again. The grossness of the separation of a child and her mother endorsed by any group of people, much less my own parents…There are no words.

Once, I texted Marley's dad to discuss how good it would be if he would cease speaking horrible things to Marley about me. His reply came quickly. *Maybe when you stop listening to rap, I'll let you see her.* Wow. Just wow. Rap is a form of music highly discouraged as a form of entertainment within the organization. It is not considered a personal issue of taste in music. But, then again, not much is left to personal taste in the organization.

It would be somewhat different if I had proven myself to be a bad parent, a drug user, a drunk. Whatever. But I just wanted to leave the organization. I wanted to marry Crystal.

And so I asked her. The summer of 2013, I made some calls and arranged for the pom squad from the local high school to go to her beauty salon. The proposal included them dancing to Bruno Mars's "Marry You." She said yes, and we were happier than I ever thought I could be. We arranged to go to New York for a November 1 wedding since gay marriage was not yet legal in the state of Oklahoma. We made the trip with two friends and planned for an Oklahoma ceremony. Nothing ever felt more normal or desired to me than to marry the woman who had come to be my best friend.

We put a wedding announcement in the paper. I listed my mother's name but chose to leave my father's name out of the announcement. He told Marley he was glad I did.

All I could hope for was that my only child would come to see the hate as just that: hate.

I began to reason in a more focused way than I ever had. I knew the Bible. I knew its comments on homosexuality. I also knew that where love is absent, God's spirit doesn't exist. There are fruits of the spirit, and from what I understand, these are visible in people who have God's blessing. The Jehovah's Witnesses I encountered over the years had many of these fruits. For instance, the fruit of God's spirit is said to yield love, kindness, patience, etc. Yet, as a whole, their policies didn't reflect their vocal beliefs in these fruits.

I still know in my heart that many Jehovah's Witnesses are just good people doing what they're told. My mother is one of those people. A mother should never feel that it is her scriptural obligation to shun her child. Nearly every day, I see someone from the local congregation in town. They always stare until I look at them, and then they look away—even Mother.

Once such instance resonated with Marley. I went to a local market to buy peaches. As I stood there, filling my bag with them, my mother walked in. Encounters had happened many times up to this point, but I wasn't as inclined to duck my head this time. I just continued making my peach selection. She didn't see me at first. Just for a brief moment, I tried to smell her. Weird, maybe, but even without perfume, my mother had a pleasant smell. Always the same. Then she noticed me. She turned and walked out the door. I watched her walk away and finished my shopping. It was a small produce market, and making selections didn't take long. I walked outside, where she sat in her van. She wanted to do her shopping but not alongside me.

I called Marley. "Marley, are you at my parents' house?" Yes. I told her of the encounter.

Not long after, my mother walked in to her home, and Marley asked her if she had seen me. "No, Marley, I didn't see her." Lie.

"OK," Marley said.

Later in the day, my mother told Marley that she had indeed seen me and wasn't sure why she had been dishonest.

Marley seemed to begin to get what I had been saying about Jehovah's Witnesses that day.

This is where it gets to me. If one is indeed carrying out the will of God, is there shame that accompanies that? I know my Bible history. Jonah, the ancient prophet chosen by God to declare righteous judgment, was scared of his assignment and thus initially ran the other direction. However, in general, prophets were bold in their assignments. So, let's just say God has sanctioned shunning. For the sake of argument, let's say this is God's chosen way of punishment for wayward sinners. Why are shunners embarrassed to tell others they do it?

One friend of mine approached my mother at a local store. She leaned in to hug her and whispered into her ear, "God would never approve of what you're doing to her." The conversation ended abruptly as my mother hurried away.

I've certainly done things I'm not proud of. But if God himself commissioned my actions on any given matter, I would proudly carry them out. I was proud to explain to people why I was visiting their homes when I participated in the door-to-door work. I was scared to be there. I was scared of their mean dogs. But I wasn't scared to tell them why I felt the need to be there. The commission at Matthew 24:14 was mine. There was an arrogance with which I carried out what I felt to be my personal commission from Jesus.

To rebel vocally against policies of the organization was considered apostasy. Apostasy by definition is an abandonment of one's faith or principles. I don't feel what I did is apostasy, then. Jehovah's Witnesses believe apostates have committed the unforgivable sin. I don't believe I've done that, either. I do renounce any religion that not only covers up the molestation of children but also, by minimizing the acts, facilitates the abuse.

That organization has been called a pedophile's paradise. No wonder. An abuser can abuse for years and years under the confidentiality rules. Even when found out, the abuser can claim repentance and be allowed to remain an active member of the congregation. Should he or she not even be repentant, he or she can be disfellowshiped for a time and then return after completing the same steps I did for immorality.

As of the time I left the Jehovah's Witnesses, there were grades of sin. Some sins were viewed as much worse than others. I now feel sin is sin. We all are guilty of varying sins. However, when a molester sins, he or she also commits a crime. The judicial committees of Jehovah's Witnesses feel well equipped to handle such occurrences without the involvement of authorities. At least, that was my experience.

The day came for the hearing in what Witnesses would call Caesar's court.

The assistant district attorney in our city met with me and two other victims. The three of us stood alone, despite numerous other victims. One of the absent victims texted me that he wished me the best of luck, but as a Witness still within the organization, he could not risk allying himself with us. Detectives had met with staunch resistance to their efforts to uncover victims.

In our meeting with the assistant district attorney just prior to the hearing, she informed us Ronnie would be present but not to worry. She told us a patrolman would be there to walk us into the courtroom. As he escorted us in, he led us directly past where Ronnie and his wife were sitting, awaiting being called in. Ronnie's wife reached out and touched one of the male victims, Tim. "I'm sorry," she said.

Crystal was with me, along with a couple of dear friends who came for support. I had no trouble staring at Ronnie. So gross. I pitied his wife but was also angry with her. It's my belief that she had known all this time.

I don't know that for a fact, but what I did know for sure was that if my child didn't want to go somewhere with someone, she wouldn't be forced. If she developed behavior problems, I would find out why. If my husband had manifested an affection for young children and frequently had them in our home, I would've known. Period.

As I looked about the courtroom, I saw my parents and several of the elders. Where else were they sitting but on the side of Ronnie.

The three of us as victims began to cry. I had heard tales of this happening—Jehovah's Witnesses siding with criminals they deemed forgiven. I must say, I hadn't really felt like that would be the case here.

We had all the documentation and proof that he had done what we said he had. My parents loved me; I was sure of it. They were just going along with this shunning business because it was their only means of bringing me to repentance. That's what I sincerely believed.

On hundreds of occasions, Crystal and I had discussed possible rationales for shunning and a parent's willingness to participate in it. Up until that moment in court, I reasoned that worldly people just didn't understand. There are rules in place for a reason, and Jehovah's Witnesses are simply demonstrating an admirable loyalty to their God and their faith. To a small degree, I still believe that to be true. However, after feeling the devastation of seeing my parents sit by a man who molested their daughter, I am emotionally done. I'm done with the filthiness that their form of worship includes. Shunning is a filthy way to teach someone a lesson. Additionally, covering up the molestation of one's own child is, in my mind, willful participation in the crime.

I was called to the stand. "Were you molested by this man?" Yes, I was. "Were you coerced into not revealing it to authorities?" Yes, I was.

My father was called to the stand. "Do you recollect, sir, Ronnie being in a position of oversight in the local congregation of Jehovah's Witnesses?"

His reply shot through me: "No, I have no recollection of that."

"Do you, sir, recollect your daughter asking to not be taken to Ronnie's home on numerous occasions?"

I was already numb from the first reply but heard him answer, "No, I don't recall that."

I gasped. *You fucking liar.* In the judicial hearings at the Kingdom Hall before Ronnie was disfellowshiped the first time, my father had recalled it. How quickly his loyalty shifted when his daughter was an expelled apostate.

In the organization, loyalty is given to anyone called a brother or a sister over one considered worldly and especially an apostate. The distinction of being called a "brother" or a "sister" only comes with becoming a baptized member of the Jehovah's Witness organization.

A few years before I left, there was a *Watchtower* article we studied as a congregation. It commented on expelled, shunned members. It stated that those members should still be loved as if they were still members, although the shunning must remain. They were to be viewed as sheep who had simply temporarily strayed from the flock.

The organization has changed its stance on that. Recently, new light has come to them from God. Expelled, shunned members should be treated as if God has already killed them.

New light is to be accepted without question, I know. But this…this is absolutely a scary, scary thing.

A friend of mine uses a Voltaire quote on her website: *Those who can make you believe absurdities can make you commit atrocities.* How true.

And it was atrocious. I felt weak at the sight of my mother and the words of my father. I would find out later that Crystal had been in the same waiting room with them at the district attorney's office, awaiting the hearing. My mother and father sat expressionless.

The judge announced that he didn't agree with the caveat on the statute of limitations and promptly dismissed the case. The assistant district attorney voiced her intent to appeal, and the judge noted it.

There we sat, watching Ronnie go free. We watched the elders file out. Were they proud of themselves? My homosexuality and apostasy had disqualified me not only as their friend and daughter but also as a human being. *I'm not the one in the wrong here. You people have some explaining to do should the Lord ever deal with you at all.*

We went to the local coffee shop with our friends, with the exception of Tim. He couldn't handle it. The anxiety showed on his face to the extent that I couldn't look at him.

This was my fault. I had dredged this up for them. I felt completely hopeless.

Hope had evaded me those past months. My child had been visiting, it seemed, only because of a court order to do so. I had her exactly half of the time, and per the court order, she wasn't allowed to visit or spend time with others without my consent. They strenuously fought me on that regularly.

The pain of it was nearly too much to bear. I saw news programs chronicling children being taken from their homes or the streets they played on. With horror, I would continue to think of these families, not knowing them but praying they would get their children back. Equally saddening were reports of families torn apart by things like cancer and murder. Separation devastates families. Yet there I was. *I'm right here. See me? Talk to me. Hug my neck. Text me. Something. I'm right here.* Many times, desperate to speak with my mother, I texted her. She blocked me from her phone.

The world, I noticed, was full of families that just wanted to be together and had been robbed of that luxury for any number of reasons. And it is a luxury. You just may not realize it until it's gone from your life.

Did they suppose this was a decision I made? Does anyone truly believe that a gay person just woke up one day and says, "I think I'll live a gay life now"? Who the hell would do that?

JW leaders hope your life is so full of misery that it will drive you back to that organization. For me, the misery *is* the organization. Yet, it took me a very long time to recognize that. Read any book on cult indoctrination, and it is clear that I was in a cult. The safety of it, the closeness and the devoutness of it, feel right. It isn't right. It takes time to know that, though.

I had done the best I knew to do for that organization. I had faltered at times but, all in all, had devoted thousands of hours trying to qualify for everlasting life and to help others do the same. Maintaining that momentum is what matters to the members. After all these years, I finally feel comfortable with the knowledge that the momentum isn't what God sees. It's my sincerest belief that he values those who can't keep up the momentum. He sees us fall time and time again and scoops us up.

I now firmly believe that God puts people in our paths to help us cope with awful things. We must slow down and take notice. We mustn't be so hardened in our belief systems that we miss them.

For twenty years, I had worked for a somewhat conservative family business. I had always been scared to discuss many of the things regarding my sexuality and religious experiences with them. From the start, though, they steadfastly had my back, no matter what was thrown at me. Even hate from others, non-JWs—they helped me to survive it. I'm grateful—so grateful. This family not agreeing with anything about Jehovah's Witnesses proved to be invaluable. As members of the Baptist faith, they offered different ways to look at things.

Spiritually, I just laid there. I did not read my Bible or pray, as Crystal did. She had a church family I did not make my own. God, for me, was a monster. He saw what happened to me and did nothing to prevent it. I knew Christ died for me, but it was an abstract idea. It was as if Jehovah's Witnesses' view of me was God's view of me. Sadly for them, I don't think that's true. I know they need to be right. I know they need to be vindicated.

But what if—just what if—they are wrong? I had never considered that a possibility. I steadfastly believed my entire life that they were correct. The only true religion on earth. The only organization being used by God, and I just couldn't measure up or be good enough. I had tried.

But now, I was straying from that belief. Straying from long-held beliefs is scary, especially if they involve God.

One night, in a puddle of tears, I texted a friend asking for advice. Her return text is priceless to me. *Baby, when you get to the end of your rope, tie a knot and hang on. This too shall pass. I can't tell you what to do. When you were born, you were given all the answers to any problem you might have. Be still and listen. God will show you the way.*

Crystal and I have become advocates for the equal treatment of all humans, regardless of race, sexuality, or socioeconomic status in life, and we live our lives that way. We set that example for Marley, who is far and away much better now with the passage of a little time.

We respect people's rights to be who they are and even to worship as they see fit. However, when it tramples on the existence of another other human being, we can't support it.

I do know for sure I met some wonderful people through the years in the organization, but I do not in any way belong with them. I worked tirelessly for various people in the congregation. I provided meals, cleaned homes for the sick, and visited the elderly. None of them will utter a word to me now.

I am right where I need to be. My wife is hands down the best person I have ever met. She survived bouts of self-loathing and the behavior that accompanies that. My family is missing out on knowing her, and that's sad. They will likely go to their graves thinking we are somehow just bad, destined for everlasting destruction.

We will find out, won't we?

The very least we can do is love the people God has put in our lives in spite their perceived sins or wrongdoings. If we can't do that, then we have a problem worse than being gay. It is the greatest of all commands. Shouldn't we be working on mastering that? Shouldn't we be mindful that when we judge someone, we have, in that moment, sinned?

As for Ronnie, he most likely has something in his background that made him what he is. In many ways, I pity him. He robbed so many of us of being the people we could've been. He, without hesitation, broke us, changed our behaviors, and damaged us. We can choose to wallow. Healing is hard work but must be done if we want to live lives above what he did.

A circuit overseer once gave a talk about a fictional sister who had been offended by another sister in the congregation. He said, "Picture in your mind's eye this offended sister coming to the Kingdom Hall and just laying down outside the front door. People arrive for meeting and step over her, but she persists in laying there." He emphasized the point that doing that would be dumb, and yet holding onto a grudge is similar. Sometimes, we get mad and just decide to lie down, as it were, to make a point. When in actuality, what is better for us is to get up.

I'm getting up.

Shun me if you like. This is my town too. I won't participate in the shunning because I no longer believe that way. And so, I waved at my mother and sister the other day. The priceless looks on their faces made me smile. I did what I wanted to—not out of hate for their treatment of me but because it's the human t hing to do.

Look away if you like. It's OK.

My life awaits.

THANK YOUS

Never could I leave it unsaid that there are thanks owed for keeping me alive through recent years.

All my love goes to Crystal and Marley, the two true loves of my life.

To my friends Shannon, Linda, Paulette and Sarah. The nights and days when it was deeply dark, you didn't let go of me and made me your family when I had none. You brought laughter when I presumed it dead in me.

To Barbara, Joe, Randy, Cindy, Sheila, Miranda and Andrea....Your support garners my indefinite gratitude.

The above mentioned persons treat others as they wish to be treated and THAT, people, is what religion should be built upon.

It has taken time to see that these relationships are pure and sincere. There are certain people still out there who will love without selfishness. What a fine gem to discover.

19294221R00075

Made in the USA
San Bernardino, CA
21 February 2015